# DEVIL WALK

## A True Story

## CLINT BYARS

Unless otherwise indicated, all Scripture quotations are taken from the *Holy Bible*, King James Authorized Version, which is in the public domain.

Emphasis within scripture quotations is the author's own.

DEVIL WALK: A True Story

ISBN: 0-924748-51-6
UPC: 88571300021-5

Printed in the United States of America
© 2005 by Clint Byars

Milestones International Publishers
4410 University Dr., Ste. 113
Huntsville, AL 35816
(256) 536-9402, ext. 234; Fax: (256) 536-4530
www.milestonesintl.com

1 2 3 4 5 6 7 8 9 10 11 / 09 08 07 06 05

# DEVIL WALK

## A True Story

# DEDICATION

This book is dedicated to my mom Eleanor Byars. You always taught me that I can do anything I put my mind to. You have always been there for me. Words can't express the appreciation I have for you. Thank you and I love you.

I also want to say a special thank you to my wife Sara Byars. Thank you for being my inspiration! This would not have been possible without you. I love you!

# CONTENTS

Introduction . . . . . . . . . . . . . . . . . . .ix

Chapter One     Downward Spiral . . . . . . . . . . . . . .1

Chapter Two     Death Realized . . . . . . . . . . . . . . . .19

Chapter Three     The Torment of Hell . . . . . . . . . . . .31

Chapter Four     Face to Face . . . . . . . . . . . . . . . . .49

Chapter Five     Jesus at the Crossroads . . . . . . . . .59

Chapter Six     Making a Deal With the Devil . . . . .69

Chapter Seven     From Darkness to Light . . . . . . . . .85

Chapter Eight     The Cross . . . . . . . . . . . . . . . . . .101

Chapter Nine     Death Obsession . . . . . . . . . . . . .113

Chapter Ten     Satan's Secret Sin . . . . . . . . . . . .127

Chapter Eleven     The Truth vs. the Lie . . . . . . . . . .141

Chapter Twelve     Choose Life . . . . . . . . . . . . . . . .157

The Truth vs. the Lie References . . .165

About the Author . . . . . . . . . . . . .169

# INTRODUCTION

─ ⊰◈⊱ ─

We live in a spiritual age. Interest in spirituality of all varieties has perhaps never been as high as it is today, especially in the west, and that interest continues to rise. People everywhere are searching for meaning and purpose in their lives. The universal questions "Who am I?" and "Why am I here?" are just as relevant to us in the 21st century as they have been to every preceding generation. Contrary to what many of us have been led to expect, none of mankind's great advances in science and technology have brought answers to those questions.

With science having failed to satisfy, many people have begun to reevaluate the spiritual dimension of man. Everyone who explores spirituality with any depth must at some point deal with the question of the supernatural. Is there a supernatural realm that is invisible to physical eyes? Does God exist? If so, can we communicate with Him? How? Is there a real, literal devil who can influence people's thoughts and actions? Are demons real? What about angels?

Most people come to terms with the idea of the existence of some kind of "higher being." But some don't. Some people flatly deny the existence of the supernatural in any way, shape or form. Others accept the reality of the spiritual realm but question its relevance to our daily lives in the physical world. Still others seek ways to connect with the spiritual world in any way they can, whether through drugs, chanting, channeling, prayer, the occult or whatever.

Without the right foundation, such exploration and self-absorbed thinking can lead into very dark places. Proverbs 3:5-6 says, *"Trust in the LORD with all thine heart; and lean not unto thine own understanding. In all thy ways acknowledge him, and he shall direct thy paths."* Whenever we try to answer life's biggest questions by mental reasoning alone—by leaning on our own understanding—we will reach the wrong conclusions. We want our answers to be simple, straightforward and easy to accept. Sure, we want to discover our true identity, but we also want it to make sense to us. We want everything to fit neatly into the paradigm that we have developed from our own life experiences.

In short, we become our own god. We carve out a way of thinking that placates our own thought processes. Out of all created beings, we humans alone have the unique ability to fashion gods in our own image and then believe in the reality of what we have fashioned for ourselves. We do all this in an effort to discover meaning for our existence. We want to know that we have some kind of purpose. After all, purpose is what drives us and motivates us to keep going.

Our search for meaning and purpose propels us eventually on a journey of self-discovery. This journey can take many forms and lead down many different paths. The path I took was one I did not deliberately choose. Unexpectedly one night I was thrust into an encounter that not only shattered everything I thought I believed, but also very nearly destroyed me. Except for the grace and mercy of God and the Lord Jesus Christ, I would not be alive today to tell the story.

It is a classic story of good versus evil that addresses the fundamental questions, "Does God exist? Is the devil real?" Before this encounter I would have answered "no" to both questions. My experience that night and in the weeks and months that followed changed my perspective forever.

The story I share in the following pages is my story—shocking, even seemingly unbelievable at times—but it is a true story. My prayer is that my story will leave you feeling incredibly empowered in the Lord Jesus Christ and forever destroy your fear of the devil. This is the story of when I met the devil *face to face*—and my subsequent journey into the face of *infinite love*.

# Chapter One

# DOWNWARD SPIRAL

—◄· ▣◊▣ ·►—

It was a night like any other night. Nothing about this night hinted that something extraordinary was about to happen. I and three of my friends were about to take a journey. The four of us, three guys and one girl, jumped in the car to go to a movie. Little did I know that this was the beginning of a ride that I would remember for the rest of my life. What happened this night would change my life forever.

Our trip actually began before we got out of the driveway because the four of us were already tripping on LSD. Even though I was under the influence of a mind-altering drug, the story I am about to relate *really happened.* The drug merely prepared my state of mind and put me in a state of extreme vulnerability.

On our way to the movie we were listening to one of our favorite bands on the radio. Music played a huge part in my life in those days. As I listened to the trance-like beat of one particular song, I slipped into a realm unlike any other place I had ever been. This was the first hint that this was not an ordinary night. I began looking around trying to find something familiar to ground myself and, as I did so, everything around me turned gray. I remember thinking that it was strangely foggy out but there was something different about this fog: It seemed to be *inside* the car.

*The fog seemed to be inside the car.*

In a matter of moments I could see nothing but haze. It was as though my eyes had blurred and been painted on the inside with a dark color. As I strained to see through the haze I began to panic. My heart raced and I was suddenly overwhelmed with fear. I was so frightened that I could not even move my head anymore. I remained in a sitting position but could not move at all; I seemed to be paralyzed.

Once again I tried to locate something familiar but could see nothing. I was able to discern that beyond the haze was nothing but blackness. Now it seemed as though I was no longer in the car but floating in the air, still paralyzed, in some kind of suspended state of being where there was no time or sound or vision or thought or comprehension. As quickly as that came about, the scene changed. The fog turned from dull gray to static similar to the kind you see on a television that has no signal. I was still scared out of my mind and had no idea what was happening.

For the first time, I heard a sound. I didn't recognize the sound so I focused in on it, trying to identify it. Many times since that night I have wondered what would have happened if I had *not* focused on that sound. Nevertheless, I remember making a distinct decision that night to listen to that muffled sound. The consequences of that decision would haunt me for months to come.

## THE SOUND OF VOICES

As I focused more intently on this muted sound, it began to grow. At first it sounded like the low growl of a lion stalking its prey. It seemed like an eternity as I waited for the sound to grow loud enough to tell what it was. Before long, I realized that this growl was not a single sound but multiple sounds. The sounds continued to grow louder and louder and as they did they became clearer.

A fresh wave of fear swept over me as I realized I was hearing *voices*. I could not yet make out what they were saying, but I could definitely tell they were voices; a multitude of voices all clamoring at once.

*I was linked to somebody else's thought processes.*

There seemed to be a tone of anticipation in these voices, as if they were waiting for something. Gradually, one distinguishable voice began to emerge. It was actually more than a voice; it was an entire set of concepts, as if I was reading someone else's mind but in my own reality. Somehow I sensed that this mind was thinking about me, but its thoughts were different from how I would usually define a thought. Rather than following a singular, linear process, these thoughts formed in my mind as complete concepts. It was like I could understand this mind's entire bizarre paradigm of how it saw life. My normal process of thought involves considering several different points before I understand and adopt an entire concept. This was different. It's hard to explain but it was as though I had become linked to somebody else's thought processes.

My focus turned from what was going on outside of me to what was now in my head. My mind was filled with thoughts and concepts and images of being stuck. I literally felt stuck. I was still unable to move and the paradigm of ideas rolling around in my head made me think I would be stuck forever. Fear gripped me again as I began to think that I might never get out of wherever I was.

## PATTERNS OF LIFE

At this time my vision changed again and I saw what looked like a television screen. As I stared at the screen, four patterns began to emerge. I immediately recognized these patterns as representing how I had lived my life up to that point. Even though there was some slight visualization involved, these patterns still came to me more as concepts I understood than as anything else.

When I say I saw patterns, they were more like sets of beliefs or ways of life. We all have patterns that we follow in our lives. Some of us cycle through our patterns every year. Some do it every week. To use an old cliché, with these patterns I saw my life flashing before my eyes. The main difference was that instead of seeing all the wonderful experiences I had had or all the people I had loved, I saw laid before me my attitudes and the ways I had dealt with situations in my life. Somehow this disembodied mind I had tapped into had connected to what was really in my heart. I knew this was *me* that was being displayed in front of me.

4

Someone was showing me what my life was really all about and I have to admit, I was not pleased with what I saw.

The first pattern brought some relief from what I had been experiencing up to this point. I was sitting in the back of a car going along for a ride. My emotions had completely changed. My fear was gone and I was experiencing the emotions that I normally would have experienced had I really been in that situation. I was simply sitting back enjoying the ride while somebody took me somewhere. This first pattern reflected much of what my life was like at the time. In those days I basically lived for the next big event, the next big party or the next big concert. I loved music and it seemed like I was always going to concerts or somewhere to hang out.

*I knew this was me being displayed in front of me.*

Seeing this first pattern forced me to confront my attitude toward life and to acknowledge the true motive behind my life: selfishness. My life was all about total self-gratification with no regard to anyone or anything else around me. I was even willing to abuse my body with illegal substances in order to attain the sense of getting away. Getting away somehow filled the void that I was experiencing. Going to "the next big event" subdued my hunger for purpose. I thought that being at a concert or a party was the most important place I could be at the time.

Does this sound like you at all? How much of your life has been about just "getting away"? How much of your life have you spent not living in the now but just looking forward to that next big thing that was going to come along? Looking back, it just doesn't satisfy, does it? There's got to be more to life than simply running from one big event to another looking for a little excitement or some kind of temporary high that will help take the edge off of a meaningless existence. Isn't there?

The more I experienced this pattern, the more I began to feel a sense of loss. I began to realize how much of my life I had wasted. As I said, my life was flashing before my eyes and I was not happy with the way I had spent it. Because I was experiencing this in a way that seemed to put me outside of my own consciousness, I was able to connect with my heart in a different way. Unfortunately, it sometimes takes extreme circumstances in our lives to reveal to us who we really are. Ours is a society where people generally do not live in the now or connect to who they really are. We seem to go through life living solely for ourselves and never even taking the time to examine what we truly want out of life.

The worst aspect of the first pattern was that I saw in my heart where I had come to accept where I was. I had accepted where my attitudes had brought me. I could feel the dying that took place in my heart as I chose to accept the fact that my life was about nothing. I had lived totally for myself with no regard for anyone else and the saddest part of all is that *I was fine with it.* I was genuinely shocked at the degree of apathy with which I accepted this revelation about myself. I remember actually feeling nauseated at realizing how little respect I had for myself.

## CONVENIENT MPD

As I watched this pattern unfold before me, I knew it was about me and my attitudes and about decisions I had made, but at the same time it seemed as though I was watching it happen to someone else. I have since learned that this mental and emotional detachment is quite common among people who have been diagnosed with Multiple Personality Disorder (MPD). One study has shown that many recovered MPDs recall periods early on in their condition where they had similar experiences to mine, where they see themselves in situations that they recognize as themselves but cannot endure the pain of the self-realization. So they create a mental or emotional framework to detach themselves from the pain. For people with MPD, that framework is another personality they develop to cope with what they are experiencing.

Many MPDs slip into this terrible state of existence as a way of escaping physical abuse or sexual abuse. Sometimes it is an attempt to deal with a deep sense of guilt. Regardless of the circumstances that propel the disorder, in many cases a deliberate decision to accept it is involved. I believe that the majority of people in our society have what I call "convenient MPD." We have ways of taking ourselves mentally to a place that allows us to do things that compromise our general state of mind; that is, the belief system that normally governs our behavior. How many times have you done something you know is wrong and justified it in your mind at the time, only to come back later and ask yourself in amazement, "How could I have done such a thing?" I know *I* have, more times than I care to admit. This kind of rationalization comes from detaching ourselves from our heart and going to a place that will allow us to compromise. I will discuss this more later.

Each facet of this four-part pattern brought to me a deeper sadness and a more real sense of how I had wasted my life. I remember thinking that I might be in this cycle forever. For the first time, thoughts of eternity came to the forefront of my mind.

## A PATTERN OF APATHY

The second pattern revealed several new truths of my life's paradigm up to this point. As the first phase passed, I found myself physically leaning forward. I was still in the backseat but something was going on up ahead. I could tell that it was serious and I knew that it had something to do with me. A sense of urgency came over me and I jumped up to see what was going on. I had the distinct feeling that something was really wrong but I didn't know what it was. It seemed to be like a wreck or some other kind of tragedy.

As I leaned forward to see what was happening, I could see nothing but gray. Straining to gather information about what my next phase of this vision would be, I again began to understand another concept. It was more like a decision that had taken place that caused such panic that everything around me began to spin into utter chaos. I was now beginning to realize that the decision I had just made about accepting where I was in life was the catalyst for the commotion.

Imagine, if you can, a riot where everyone is beginning to spin more and more out of control. A riot is much like a forceful wave in the ocean. As we saw in December of 2004 with the tragic tsunami in the Indian Ocean, a wave can create incredible damage. The initial rising of such a wave may appear deceptively harmless until it reaches its peak and releases all its concentrated energy in a devastating surge of destruction and loss of life.

The whirlwind that was going on around me was exactly the same. It began with feelings of confusion and panic that soon escalated to overwhelming waves of sheer terror. I could hear the voices again. They seemed to have grown in number and were now yelling and screaming as if for the sole purpose of adding to the confusion. I regained my bearings and found that I was still in the seated position leaning forward in anticipation. Like before, I was now stuck in that position. No matter how hard I tried, I could not move. It was like I was in a prison for my mind. My sense of panic would not subside.

*It was like I was in a prison for my mind.*

As with the first phase of this experience, I again reached a point where I had to make a decision, and that decision deepened the sadness I was experiencing about my life. Once again I decided to accept where I was. I have often wondered what would have happened if I had chosen not to accept what was going on. Would I have snapped out of it or was this an appointment with destiny that I could not escape?

What decision are you facing? More importantly, what are you doing about it? Are you choosing to take control of your path or are you sitting back and letting your previous mistakes rule your life?

I believe that in this situation if I had chosen to stop the vision, I would have come to my right mind. But I didn't, and so the nightmare continued. Once again I found myself accepting how pathetic my life was and once again was shocked at the willingness I displayed in accepting where I had found myself. Although I've never faced jail time, I can imagine that my situation was similar to the feelings of a murderer in a courtroom. He knows he is guilty and that no matter the verdict of the jury, he will have to live with what he has done for the rest of his life. That's how I felt. I knew I was where I was because of myself. No one else was to blame. It was totally my doing and, again, somehow I was fine with it. In my detached MPD-like way, I was amazed at my capacity simply to not care. Although I fully accepted the fact that I was responsible for wasting my life, I still chose to accept it with little apprehension.

Imagine driving in your car through a residential neighborhood. You're listening to your favorite song without a care in the world. Suddenly, a small child runs out in front of your car. Unable to stop or turn in time, you end up hitting the child. Now imagine getting out and looking at the child's lifeless body lying under your car and realizing that in your heart you don't even care that you took this child's life. Callously, you get back in your car and drive off with no regard for the victim's family or what might happen to you for leaving the scene.

Such a scenario may seem morbid and unthinkable, but it perfectly illustrates the decision I had made about myself. How could I possibly have sunk to the level where I placed no value on life, either my own or anybody else's? All I know is that such was the severity of the decision I made about myself. Seeing how little value I had for life, I had the opportunity to change it, but instead I did nothing. I simply accepted my lack of self-worth. I even threw my head back in a defiant gesture as if to say, "I don't care."

I have since worked a lot with troubled teenagers and have seen this same attitude over and over. I have seen their extreme lack of self-worth and it saddens my heart. The personal experience I am describing is the most extreme of the extreme, but the principle is no different from that in many people's lives. Dr. Jim Richards has said that the number one disease of our society today is a lack of self-worth. In a later chapter I will discuss more about self-worth and how we can overcome the negative and self-defeating beliefs we have adopted about ourselves.

## PATTERNS OF DESPAIR AND HOPELESSNESS

Throwing my head back in defiance at the second pattern actually brought on the third pattern. This pattern eerily described the way I had been making decisions in life. I realized that I had some degree of control over what was going on, but I just blew it off, much as I had done all my life. I continued to minimize the seriousness of my attitude and actions and, bereft of any sense of personal dignity or character, I threw my head to the left and said, "Forget it!"

As soon as I said those words I found myself sitting back in the backseat again, but this time I was leaning to the left. I can remember having the attitude that nothing mattered and that I was just going to kick back and cruise through life staying as disconnected as possible. Leaning back seemed to me to be my justification for the way I had just handled the previous situation.

I was now caught in a cycle that continually revealed to me my apathy toward life and the self-serving and self-destructive attitudes I had formed based on my decisions. My life, or at least how I had managed my life, was passing before my eyes. I have heard of people having near-death experiences where their life passed before their eyes, but this was nothing like that. This experience left me so disappointed and so discouraged that I felt what little shred of life I did have left begin to slip away. As my will for living slid into the abyss, I physically slumped back, leaning to the left. This led to the fourth and final pattern.

In the fourth pattern I realized that I really didn't care about anything. But as I sat in that slumped position a strange thing happened: A tiny spark of hope began to burn inside me. This was hard to believe given what I had just accepted about myself. How could this be possible? How could I feel what I was feeling? I found myself suddenly back in the first position of this vision, sitting back leaning slightly to the right as I had been when this whole bizarre experience began. I actually began to have a little hope. I started to get excited at the thought that this whole ordeal might be over. It was as though I had awakened from a nightmare to find myself back in the car going to the movie with my friends.

A quick look around dashed all my hopes as I realized this was far from the truth. Quickly and uncontrollably, I leaned forward just as I had before. Again I experienced that same panic and terror that I had the first time I was in that position. Just as quickly, my head snapped over to the left as if to signify that I didn't care. While in this position I re-experienced my absolute lack of self-worth and value for life that I had earlier accepted. And just like before, I leaned

12

back in utter despair, accepting the dying that took place from acknowledging my reality.

## CAUGHT IN THE CYCLE

Like a feedback loop these four patterns repeated in a circular motion for what seemed an eternity. I was stuck in a seemingly endless cycle of hope, apathy, defiance and despair. Unable to stop myself, I kept leaning to the right in interest of living, jumping up and still leaning to the right in interest of what was coming up ahead, seeing the situation that sparked my interest but blowing it off, throwing my head to the left in defiance of life and making the decision to be my own person, and finally leaning back to the left in a state of utter hopelessness. Then it all began again.

My head circled around and around mimicking the four-pattern cycle in which I was stuck. To an outside observer, my repeated motion of rolling my eyes and throwing my head back would have communicated the attitude of "Who cares?" In this state I had to face the harsh reality that I had gone through virtually my entire life showing little interest in anything. Anything I *had* shown interest in or tried to commit myself to eventually fell away because somewhere in the midst of it all I had blown it off in a defiant decision that I needed to be my own person.

As this circular motion continued, the feeling returned that I would be stuck in this cycle forever. For the first time that night the word *hell* came into my mind. The idea formed in my head that this cycle of hope-apathy-defiance-despair would never end and that pattern would be my personal hell. I had been given a chance to evaluate my life but

13

*for the first time that night the word hell came into his mind* did nothing to change it. I simply accepted it as my reality, and now it looked like it would be my eternal reality.

Looking back, it amazes me how quickly I accepted my "fate." With hardly a care I yielded myself to the idea of "going through the motions" in an eternal mockery of how I had lived my life. I did try to break the cycle a few times, but the effort to stop myself from moving in that circular pattern was so great that I quickly gave up. This was my hell and I was fine with that. Something in my brain told me I was getting what I deserved.

*For the first time that night the word "hell" came into my mind.*

I remember thinking that I could never stop the cycle no matter what I did. The cycle seemed to continue for so long that I actually began to get used to it. At one point I actually made the decision to *stay* in the pattern. It wasn't difficult; I would just keep spinning my head around forever. I was so comfortable with the notion of not caring about anything that I was willing to stay in that pattern for eternity. The moment I finally made that determination, the cycle stopped.

## OWNING OUR "STUFF"

Suddenly, I was back in control of my body and still in the backseat of the car. I later described what I had gone through at this point to the people I was with and they told me I was "out of it" for only about 30 seconds.

It's amazing how quickly we can bring ourselves to a place where we are willing to accept the worst possible scenario!

Instead of taking control of our thought patterns, we get caught in a cycle of self-destructive and self-defeating thoughts and behavior that doom us to a life of repeating the same mistakes over and over. At some point we simply settle in and say, "This is the way I am" and throw our emotional involvement in life into cruise control. The moment we "check out" emotionally, we remove the safeguards on our decision-making capability and set ourselves up to make repeated destructive decisions.

Psychologists call these patterns "schemas." A schema is best understood as a groove in our brain much like a ditch or rut that water naturally flows through. It's as if we switch our brains to automatic pilot and are taken for a ride over which we have no control. This in turn eats away at our self-worth and self-acceptance until we begin to believe that the negative circumstances and destructive situations in our lives are simply what we deserve. Even if we want to break the cycle, we often cannot in our own strength because our efforts to break the cycle repeatedly fail, reinforcing our lack of self-worth and sense of deserving what we've got, thus dragging us even deeper into the grip of the cycle.

Have you ever found yourself experiencing a hint of victory but then deciding that it is too difficult to continue fighting? Maybe you're actually *afraid* of victory because of how your life would change. Maybe you tell yourself you deserve the quality of life you're experiencing. Maybe you just don't think life is worth participating in, so you just cruise through. Maybe you don't know that there is any other way to live. After all, if you make a decision to overcome a certain problem area of your life, how will you do it? Where will you get the strength? Maybe you don't even know there is a better way of life available.

The principle I came away with in accepting that the cycle I was stuck in was all my doing, something I had created in the way I had lived my life, was that the minute I owned responsibility for it, it stopped. That is so true in life. Merely owning responsibility for your negative thought and behavioral patterns may not make them stop, but it will give you some measure of strength over them. You have to realize where you are before you can get to where you want to be.

*When we choose to step out of denial is when real freedom can come.*

There is incredible freedom in admitting our problems to ourselves. When we choose to step out of denial is when real freedom can come. Once we accept where we are, we have clear sight to see where we want to go with our lives. Once we admit to ourselves where we are and honestly own our dysfunction, we then gain power over it. We still have to deal with the consequences of how we have been living or treating people, but now we have this sense of renewed power. Owning our "stuff" may not automatically change our relationships or life situations, but it is the first step to walking out of the power it has over us. There is a Chinese proverb that says, "We have to *be* a thing before we can *not* be that thing." Taking responsibility for our own attitudes and behavior means being brutally honest with ourselves. Only then can we move toward change and freedom.

## DOWNWARD SPIRAL OF DEATH AND HELL

In my case, owning responsibility for my life choices

When we chose to step out of denial is when real freedom can come.

ended the cycle, but that didn't mean my vision was over. It simply entered a new phase.

As I became aware that I was in the car, I looked toward the front and saw what looked like letters inside a spiral. This swirling mass in front of me resembled the fog that had surrounded me earlier, but this time it was spiraling counterclockwise in front of me. The center of the spiral was very dark, the way I imagine a black hole in space would be: a collapsed star with a gravitational pull so great that not even light can escape. As I continued to stare into the spiral, the letters became clearer and I saw that they spelled the word *DEATH*! The letter "D" was the largest and the others got progressively smaller as they were drawn deeper into the abyss in front of me. The letters swirled around in a manner that reminded me of a sick horror movie. In fact, the mood of my surroundings began to darken and become heavier and heavier until I began to feel like I was trapped in a horrible movie with no hope of escape.

As I watched the letters float eerily around I again heard voices. They seemed to be celebrating as if they had accomplished a great task. This time, however, they weren't in my head but very distinctly came from outside of me. I could not see the source of these voices but there was no mistaking that they were real. The excited tone of the voices stirred in me a deeper state of fright and torment. I was still watching the letters and listening to the voices when the word *HELL* joined the word *DEATH* in the dark, nightmarish spiral in front of me. While the letters forming the word *DEATH* were dull and cold-looking, the letters for *HELL* were tinged with a hint of blood red.

17

I cannot adequately describe in words how demented and frightening this thing in front of me looked. I'm not even sure its appearance disturbed me as much as the emotions that it stirred up in me. For the first time, I began to have the sense that I was dying. Thoughts of death became very prevalent in my mind at this point. I got the frightening sense that this was my "death trip." The shouts and screeches that were drowning out all other noises were backing up that very idea. Since I didn't know what to expect from death except from what I was seeing and hearing around me, everything that was happening to me seemed to point to one cold, harsh reality: *I was dying.*

# Chapter Two

# DEATH REALIZED

In a moment, I was back in the car with my friends. What I had just seen and experienced simply came to a stop, leaving me with a sense of confusion beyond anything I had ever faced.

An LSD trip has a point called "the peak" where you basically go insane. LSD slows your brain functions and renders you unable to experience what is going on around you in real time. You are still moving in real time but your mind can't keep up. That's why people claim to "figure things out" on an acid trip. What really happens is that you focus on something internal so intently that you notice every facet of it. One person may ponder the purpose of existence and come out of the trip with "a revelation." Another person may stare at their fingernails all night and be amazed at how they just keep growing. Whatever you focus on is intensified under LSD. I say that simply as an indication of how confusing an acid trip can be. I had tripped many times before this night, but I had never faced the kind of confusion that now swirled in my brain.

While whirling in this altered state I began to think about what had just happened. How could I have such a negative attitude about life? How could I be so apathetic? How could I have let my life spin so far out of control that I would even be asking myself these questions?

I thought back over my life. I really wasn't such a bad kid. I never got in any real trouble. I was on the wrestling team in high school and was pretty decent at that. I had good friends and good relationships with most of my family. I had good grades all through school. All in all, I was a pretty decent kid. I simply could not accept the idea that my life was in the state it was in.

As I pondered these thoughts, I heard the voices again. They were reaffirming what I had just gone through and reminding me of how pathetic my attitude was. It seemed they were determined to keep me stuck in that area. In my weakened mental state I was open to anything they had to say. I didn't even question what they were impressing upon me. These voices bombarded me with statements like, "You deserve this"; "This is your fault"; "You'll never change"; "You'll always be this way"; "You'll never escape." As I listened to these accusations the voices became louder and louder until they were as loud as my own thoughts and as loud as anything else going on around me. Actually, they must have been louder than anything else because those voices are all that I remember being able to hear.

By now I was feeling extremely depressed and drained and I looked over at the person to my right. I was very close with this person. I was once again aware of all three people in the car with me and I just looked at them. My vision was blurry and I still had a haze over my eyes that seemed to paint everything a pale color, like the color of death. Staring at the person in the backseat with me, I realized that I knew him and yet he was unexplainably different. He looked the same but somehow he was not the same person. He didn't try to speak but just stared at me with a strange smile on his face that deepened the fear that was already steadily mounting in my heart. His face conveyed the notion that something was very wrong. As I looked more intently, his expression seemed more and more sadistic. His smile conveyed the idea that he had complete power over me, like a madman gazing at his next victim, looking forward to the pleasure he was going to get out of hurting me. The more I looked at his twisted expression, the more my fear grew.

## AN UN-HUMAN PRESENCE

Just then I noticed the song that was playing on the radio. It was a droning, hypnotic song with lyrics that eerily fit my situation. I don't remember the exact words, but the gist of the song was someone going into the depths of my soul. It spoke of someone having control over me and how they would be there from that point on. I remember thinking that there was nothing I could do about it. I had slipped into this realm's control and I could never leave. Obviously, I was very confused about what was happening. I felt like I was still in a movie and there was about to be a major shift in the plot. I sensed that something significant was coming, but I had no control over it. My thoughts and emotions were consumed with what was about to happen.

At this point the voices were silent but I knew they were still there. In this shift of consciousness, the voices began to take on a different role. Now they were no longer just voices. There was more to them than I had earlier realized. They started to take on more significance. I now felt as if some kind of being, some kind of personality, was behind the voices. As I focused my attention on the origin of the voices, I got the strange but definite sense that they were not human. Do you know how you can tell when someone walks up behind you or you're sleeping and you can feel your child standing at the foot of your bed? I had that same kind of sensation, yet at the same time it was different. A presence was near at hand, and that presence was not human. The voices were more than just voices, and they were of distinctly unearthly origin.

*Some kind of personality was behind the voices.*

My mind raced as I tried to understand what this could be. I thought about ghosts but I didn't believe in ghosts. Actually, at that time in my life I didn't believe in anything other than what I could see and feel and touch. I had no real Christian upbringing and didn't even believe in God. So at the moment I had no explanation; I just knew I wasn't hearing the voices of *people.*

## BETWEEN TWO PLANES OF EXISTENCE

As I looked back at this person seated next to me, his presence made me feel the same way the other beings did.

This person looked like my friend, but was he really? So much was happening in my mind that I could not keep up. *He looks like the guy I know*, I thought, *but why do I think he's not?* I realized then that I was slipping into some other kind of realm. I felt like I was between two separate planes of existence. Everything looked familiar but seemed artificial. All the people in the car looked like people I knew, yet I suspected they were imposters. What was going on? How could I be in another state of existence yet everything looked the same? At that time in my life I was into various kinds of New Age thought and the only thing I could come up with was that I had somehow slipped into some kind of parallel universe.

I don't remember if the creatures told me this or if I figured it out myself, but I finally realized I was slipping into hell. Thoughts of death consumed me. Once again incredible terror overwhelmed me as I thought I was dying and going to hell. But was this what hell was really like? As I said, I had no real Christian upbringing. I had never opened a Bible. Except for a few times at Easter when I was little, I had never been to church. So I had no idea what to expect from hell.

My confusion mounted even more. *If I'm going to hell*, I thought, *why does everything look the same?* I tried to connect to something that was real or that would snap me out of this, but everything around me only thrust me deeper into the reality that I was going to hell. Since I had no idea what to expect of hell, and since everything around me seemed to confirm my feelings, I concluded that this indeed must be what hell was like.

At this point I began to believe that my surroundings were no longer real. I was no longer with my friends in the car even though it looked like I was. This was not my reality but only a copy of what I knew. This copy, which looked like a picture on a television with poor reception, was distinctly hellish.

## DEMONS IN THE CAR?

I looked to the front of the car and the two people up there were different too. In my mind this whole new reality began to unfold and progress. As I struggled to hold on to some form of sanity, I began to think of these creatures in the background as demons. The moment I did, the idea clicked in my mind. Of course they were demons; it was perfectly logical. Immediately the voices confirmed in my mind that these creatures that looked like my friends were actually demons. I was in an alternate reality and my mind was experiencing some kind of residual imaging of what my life had looked like before.

By now, I was fully convinced that I had passed completely into this altered state of existence. There were times in the night when everything came to a halt. During these times I was allowed to reflect on what had just happened. It's like I was given the opportunity to process what I was experiencing. Even though I occasionally felt that I was given time to myself, I soon realized that these demons never left my side for a second. At this point the demons were no more than about four or five feet from me. I could literally feel their presence. Even though I could not yet see them, I was fully aware that they were there. Somehow I sensed that there were seven or eight demons communicating with me, but it felt as if all of hell was in the background watching me.

This group of demons seemed drawn to me, almost as if I was a magnet attracting them. I still could not discern them with my eyes, but I began to be able to see them in my mind. They were about two or three feet tall and kind of slumped over. Their flesh was gray and bumpy and rough and quite cold. As I became aware of their hands, which were like gnarled claws, I felt very afraid that at any moment they would start tearing at my flesh.

*These demons never left my side for a second.*

This gang of demons was constantly agitated and panicky as if they were angry. This only made me feel more nervous and afraid. All their attention was focused on me, and they seemed determined to keep all the hellish thoughts and ideas of death in the forefront of my mind. From this point on I believed and accepted anything they said. They reaffirmed that I was trapped, that I was never getting away, and that I would be with them forever.

Abject, mindless fear gripped my heart. Hopelessness and utter despair swept over me like a tidal wave. I was embarrassed and utterly ashamed that my life had fallen to this point. No words could ever adequately describe the empty feeling I had inside. It was as if I was suspended over the "black hole" of emptiness in my soul and saw hell inside. It felt so deep. The accusation kept coming back to me that this is what I deserved.

Whenever those kinds of thoughts hit me, I actually slumped down myself. The demons seemed to be able to read my body language and tell what I was thinking. I never got the sense that they could read my mind, but they definitely knew what I was experiencing. Thinking back on it, they were like a team with a single purpose, working together with such cohesiveness that at times they came across as one voice. They knew what they were there for and they were not going to stop.

Visually, I still could not really see anything around me. I remember trying to look out the window but could see nothing. At times my vision would clear for a moment and I would actually recognize where I was, but it quickly clouded over again, leaving me with nothing to focus on except what I was hearing.

## DEATH ANTICIPATED

As before, as if in a movie, I could feel a plot change coming. The tension increased yet another degree, and the creatures around me sensed it too. They knew exactly what was coming. The demons began to get very excited as if this is what they had been waiting for. I felt as though they were clawing each other to get a closer view. They drew in closer to me, within about two to three feet. Relentlessly they kept pounding away at how I was going to spend eternity with them. It's hard to describe, but their bodies seemed to tense up like a body builder flexing his muscles. They were proud of what was happening and what they were doing to me.

I became aware again of the feeling that all hell was watching. In addition to the now familiar demonic voices, I could hear roars in the background. The voices kept repeating, "Here it comes! Here it comes!" These demons seemed to take great satisfaction out of creating more fear in me. They seemed to take extreme pleasure in watching my anxiety level rise as a result of their words. I was so frightened that I just put my head down and clenched into a ball. Every muscle in my body tensed. It was almost as if they were counting down. With increasing excitement they kept saying, "Here it comes! Here it comes!" In a flash of insight I realized that they were anticipating my death. They were so elated over my approaching death that they actually were having a celebration!

*All of hell seemed to be watching.*

I was still curled up in a ball. All of a sudden, I looked up and the person in the passenger seat, who I believed to be a demon, looked back and grabbed my leg. In reality, my friend was just checking on me but I did not see it that way. This person was no longer my friend but a demon that looked like my friend; a demon that was just as determined to see me die as the rest of the beings. I quickly looked over at the person next to me and, sure enough, he was one too. I was alone in this altered state of existence with nowhere to turn. The driver was swerving all over the road with the music blaring. It all resembled a very bad movie...except that it was real.

I shut my eyes, lowered my head again and held my breath. My heart was racing and all I could think about was how painful this was going to be. My fear was so intense and all-consuming that I think, if my heart had been a little weaker, I might actually have died from a heart attack.

The excitement of the demons reached its climax and they were all but dancing with anticipation. I knew what was happening; *this was my death.* Thoughts of the pain and horror of hell consumed my mind. I had visions of being burned and bitten by these creatures. A great sucking feeling in my soul left me completely empty on the inside. In a tone of insanity, the demons blurted out, "Here it is! Here it is! This is your death! Now you're dead!" Paralyzed with fear, I expected the worst. Finally, I opened my eyes, expecting the worst. For one thing, I expected to see these devils more clearly but, oddly enough, everything looked the same. I was still in the car and still seeing everything through that snowy haze.

## CROSSING OVER

As I opened my eyes, I heard the voices talking about what a good job I had done. The person next to me reached over and put his hand on my shoulder. He, as well as all the other surrounding demons, seemed proud of the way I had handled "death." They actually seemed impressed. I thought I heard my backseat companion say, "We've never seen anyone handle it that well." I definitely heard that but I couldn't tell if it was coming from him or from the demons around me. I don't know if they were trying to feed my ego or what, but they continued to discuss how well I had crossed over.

At once I detected a change in the tone of their voices. Instead of being accusatory, they now sounded accepting. Now that I had passed into hell, they almost tried to befriend me. Once they saw that I had accepted the new reality they had laid out for me, their attitude totally changed. I hadn't expected this. I had expected to drop into a place of flames and torment, but that didn't happen.

Up until this point, the voices had been random and even faint at times. Now they were as clear as if they had become a part of me. After all, now that I was dead and fully in their realm, why shouldn't I be able to hear them better? A dynamic was at work much like the one I described earlier. Now that I accepted my new reality, the truths of that reality became clearer. From this point on the voices dictated my reality and had total control of what I experienced. I was still in control of my body and basic decision-making, but I saw everything through the veil of what these demons told me.

For the first time, the demonic voices I was hearing appeared to be coming clearly from the other three people in the car. As I have already said, I in fact no longer viewed them as people but as demons themselves. I still could not tell whether it was they or the "real" demons who were telling me that I was dead. Regardless of who said it, I was keenly aware of where I now was. My new reality was not even real, but it was my reality.

*I was dead and in hell.*

Chapter Three

# THE TORMENT OF HELL

⊶ ⊞◊⊟ ⊷

Once again I was allowed time to reflect on what had just happened. The demonic activity going on was mind-numbing. I could no longer distinguish between my own thoughts and those of the demons speaking into my mind. Their words kept my focus right where they wanted it: on the conviction that I was now dead and in hell. They still played tricks with my ego, repeating the fact that no one had ever died like that before—as if they wanted me to be proud of myself! They led me to think that I must be very strong to have endured my point of death like that. I was in such a warped and weakened mental state that they actually succeeded in making me feel proud of how I had handled that moment. The demons were so convincing that I accepted their words as the product of my own thought processes.

I still had the sense that hundreds—perhaps thousands—of them were watching me. It's like they were on the edge of a deeper level of hell but could still see what was going on. I could not see all of them with my eyes, but I had a strong mental picture of what their realm looked like. I had not yet descended as low as the rest of the demons, but I knew they were present. They seemed unable to rise higher than they were, even though they wanted to. The seven or eight that were in my immediate presence were the only ones I could hear distinctly; the lower ones sounded muffled, like the far-away crowd at a football game. Their multitude of voices combined into an indistinguishable buzzing. It was very dark where they were. They were surrounded by the same smoky fog that I had seen at the beginning of this nightmare.

As I was given time to notice my observers and ponder the reality of my new surroundings, I grew more and more frightened. The only way I can describe it is to liken it to the feeling you get when someone threatens your life. I literally felt like I was staring my murderer in the face while he killed me and there was absolutely nothing I could do about it. My soul felt non-existent. There was a continual vacuum in my heart, as though there was a hole just below the surface of my skin that sank all the way down past where my host of demonic observers was. It felt like at any moment my entire body would be sucked into this hole and I would slip uncontrollably down into the void. I actually jumped in my seat trying to escape the feeling of falling. Over and over I shook myself and shifted in my seat trying to shake that feeling.

My terror was overwhelming. At times my lungs felt so constricted that I could not breathe. I've heard descriptions of how an asthma attack can reach the point where a person's lungs close completely. That is how my chest felt. A sense of panic would grasp my emotions so suddenly and so strongly that I thought I would die. Just when I thought I would die from suffocation, I remembered I was already dead. Reaching that conclusion left me more frightened than anything else I had faced up to this point. I thought, *If I'm dead, how in the world can I die again?* The words crept out of my mouth, "I don't want to die again."

My new guides must have picked up on that and run with it because now my thoughts were consumed with dying over and over. The demons began almost to chant in unison the idea of dying multiple times. I started to think how this could transpire. What would it be like to die over and over? My mind was completely consumed with thoughts of repeated death.

## ON THE HIGHWAY TO HELL

I could feel my mind starting to lose control...and just then I felt a hand on my shoulder. I looked over and the demonic copy of my friend next to me was smiling at me. But it was not a smile of comfort. In my state, his face again looked like that of a madman. His eyes conveyed the reality that I was his and I was not going anywhere. I felt like a caged pet that was about to be tormented. Quickly, I looked to the front of the car as if for support from my other two friends, but the looks on their faces were exactly the same.

My three friends appeared to me like a sick and twisted bunch of creatures that were my new guides in this hellish reality and their job was to drive me to hell. Never at any time did the thought occur to me that this just might be a bad acid trip, for it was all so real. As we drove further down the road, the voices still confirmed repeatedly that I had died and gone to hell. At this point in the night I was fully convinced of what they were telling me.

The voices seemed to be coming from the people I was with, yet their lips weren't moving. They appeared to have the ability to communicate with me without speaking. When I looked at them I could tell exactly what they wanted me to know. When they did speak, they said things like, "Are you all right?" and "What's happening?" To me, that simply added to the torment. I didn't realize that the people I was with were actually concerned about me. Still fully convinced they were demons, I thought they were making fun of me. I was scared and depressed and in despair and thought that they just wanted to rub it in.

*I felt like a caged pet that was about to be tormented.*

I tried to talk to them at times, but that only seemed to make them angry. When I said that I was dying or that I was in hell, they looked very disappointed. They even acted surprised. I quickly caught on that this was just part of the game the demons were playing with me.

I remember becoming very angry with these demons that looked my friends. I despised this twisted game, but they would not relent. They pressed more and more. The more they tried to get me to talk, the angrier I became. I felt like killing them, but what good would that do? I could not kill a demon; no one can kill a spirit being. All I could do was stare at them and despise what they were trying to do. I lowered my head and gazed at them with a wild stare. I could tell my mind was unstable because I kept wanting them to be real. Two of these people I had known most of my life, and I just wanted to talk to them. I just wanted to reach over and have a normal conversation with them. But the voices were always there to remind me that I was dead. There was no sense in trying because these were not real people.

The team of eight demons that apparently were "assigned" to me were so crafty in the points they kept going back to. They must have been able to read the looks on my face because every time I started to raise a question they talked about and affirmed the very thing I was going to ask. The eight of them maneuvered like a well-oiled machine. They were so effective, it seemed like they had been doing it for thousands of years. My personal devils were hell-bent on establishing a new (although false) reality for me, and they would not give up.

## REVERSE MATRIX

At this point I was about four hours into a year-long nightmare. Thinking back, I am amazed at how easy it was for me to accept my new reality. My emotions were elevated to an unbearable level at that time. Everything I saw and heard was backed up by everything I felt as well. By now, I knew there was no turning back. Not only was I dead and in hell, but also I faced the very real possibility of having to die over and over again, each time more painful and terrifying than the last.

Everything that had happened up to this point had taken place in the car. I looked out the window and realized that we were back at my neighborhood. Everything looked the same and yet different.

I am reminded of the scene in the movie *The Matrix* where Morpheus and Trinity first take Neo back into the

Matrix. In that sci-fi world, artificial intelligence-equipped machines take over the world and create a computer program for human minds. The reality is that people are plugged into this mainframe where their minds are alert. Their minds are all connected to this central mainframe and in their minds they live out their lives in an artificial reality while their bodies are actually in pods and used to generate power for the machines. A group of people who have escaped into the real world help people wake up from the Matrix. They have to remain hidden from the machines but enter the mainframe (the Matrix) mentally through computer connections to help others escape.

Neo's first time back in the Matrix after waking up is confusing for him. In one scene he is riding down a city street and recognizes a noodle shop he used to frequent. His brain has trouble processing that the noodle shop he knows so well isn't even real.

As we pulled back into my own neighborhood, I was in a reverse position from Neo. It was like I had been captured from the real world and plugged into the Matrix. I was seeing things that used to be real but were now only copies. It was a real puzzle. Why would hell look like my neighborhood and my old life? That was a question I pondered for several hours.

## BACK IN THE OLD NEIGHBORHOOD

By the time we got back to the house, my new reality was in full force. Somehow the house looked darker. In fact, everything around me looked darker and tinged with a sinister evil. Sure, it was nighttime, but I had never seen a night as black as this. As the car pulled into the driveway and came to a stop, my mind was now racing. *What's going to happen now? Will we open the door to the house and fall into a lower part of hell? Will the rest of the demons waiting for me down there attack me and tear at me and pull me even lower?* With every depressing and horrifying thought, my mind made the emotions very real.

Have you ever woken up from a nightmare and had to take a few minutes to convince yourself that it was only a dream? I tried to do that on this night, but the nightmare would not go away. I had continual thoughts and visions of different ways I could slip into other, more sadistic realms of hell.

We got out of the car and stood outside for a time. The night air actually felt good in my lungs. It was a welcome change to get out of what had felt like a prison. I did not think I was free, but being outside at least eased some of the mental torture that I had just endured. I tried hard to grasp some kind of reality with my mind. It was so confusing because my surroundings were so familiar. I had lived in this neighborhood for years. I knew every tree and every bump in the road. Nearby was this one tree that we used to climb as kids. If we climbed high enough, we could actually see the dog food plant in the next town.

My thoughts turned to my life and the people I knew. That provided a new angle about the reality that I was dead. How would my death affect my family? What would it do to Mom when she learned that her son died from a drug overdose? Suddenly, I felt terribly and incredibly ashamed for what I had done. Not only had I thrown my life away, I would be the cause of tremendous emotional pain for my family.

For the first time that night I began to cry at the thought of how much pain Mom would be in. I was so sorry. At that moment all I wanted was to call her and talk to her and tell her how much I loved her and that everything was okay. But the cold reality set in that everything was *not* okay. I would never see Mom again. I was dead and gone and was never coming back. The only thing I had to look forward to was eternity in hell.

*I cringed at the thought of being tortured forever.*

That set me thinking about eternity and how long eternity actually is. Until this night, I didn't believe in an afterlife. I believed that our bodies died and that was it. I had this crazy notion that our energy was absorbed by the cosmos and we simply ceased to exist. Now I cringed at the thought of being tortured forever. On top of that was the incessant idea of having to die again and again, which would be a dominant theme in my mind for many months to come.

As we walked into the house, the gray haze was still in front of my eyes. I was in such a state of shock that my mind and body simply followed the other people (demons as I saw them) without any hesitation. Somewhere in the next few moments I really began to think about what was happening to me and what it meant. By this time I was so convinced that I never even questioned whether it was real. All my thoughts were consumed with my new "reality," particularly on what "forever" in hell was going to be like. At the same time I was still extremely confused. I could not make sense of anything that was being said to me. Granted, I was on LSD, but I was at the point in the trip where basic reasoning usually returned, allowing me to think close to normal.

Not this time—and that is when the torment really began.

## DEMONIC MIND GAMES

The degree of demonic activity I was experiencing by this point was astonishing. They were working very hard to keep me in the frame of mind that I was in hell. I didn't get the sense that they necessarily enjoyed what they were doing, as if it was some kind of party atmosphere for them. Rather, their mood struck me as extremely serious. They were willing to use anything and everything to keep the reality of hell in the forefront of my mind. It's hard to describe the mental torment and game playing that these demons engaged in, partly because the thoughts and ideas are disturbing to remember, but it's more important to understand how serious the devil is about deceiving us and his willingness to use any trick, any scheme, any lie, anything he can to do it.

Walking in the house I got the sense that I was being ushered into my next prison. This prison would prove to be even more torturous than the previous. I was still profoundly aware that this vast host of demons below our current realm was watching. It made me feel like a movie character being ridiculed by the audience. As I walked through the kitchen and into the living room, I could hear the voices making fun of me. They said I should have been a comedian because my life had been such a joke. Relentlessly, over and over they poured scorn and ridicule on my head, continually beating down whatever was left of my self-worth and self-image.

I felt like they were trying to shame me to the point where I would just give up on any glimmer of hope that might be left in me. Their goal was to tear me completely down and leave me without a shred of dignity. I have to admit, it was working. They succeeded in stripping me of any kind of self-respect or sense of personal value that I could possibly have had left. Stripped of all dignity and self-worth and at the very bottom emotionally, I was fully convinced that I was in the only condition I deserved to be in: dead and in hell.

## BILLIARD BALLS AND LIGHTNING BOLTS

It was such a shock to find myself in hell. Just a few hours before, I hadn't even believed in hell or heaven or God or any kind of afterlife. In fact, I was so persuaded in my own belief system that I would have argued with anybody about it. I was so smug in my certainty that there were no such things as devils, God or any kind of spiritual realm, yet here I was right in the middle of it. The odd thing is that I accepted it right away. It was so real; I was hearing it, feeling it and communicating with it.

Something jogged my memory and reminded me of a particular conversation I had once with one of my friends. We were playing pool in the basement of my house and began philosophizing about life. In particular, we talked about how stupid people were. He and I laughed at how people waste their lives getting stuck in the system of everyday life. We thought the idea of waking up, going to work and coming home only to do the same thing all over again the next day was asinine. Our philosophy was to live life to the fullest and have as much fun as possible. Pretty simple (and bone-headed), but that was it.

We agreed that living a long life was pointless. Why live a long life of boredom? It would be much better, we concluded, to die early and go out in a blaze of fun and glory than to live a mundane life over many years. Now, in the midst of my own personal hell, I reflected back on that moment in my life and felt deep regret. How stupid I was! How messed up could I have been to want to trade a full life for a short time of fun? The "fun" we were referring to almost always included some kind of drug or party. I realized now, much too late, I thought, what an empty life that was. Once again the realization hit me like a blow to the stomach that I was the sole reason I was now in hell and there was nothing I could do about it.

Then I remembered something else my friend and I talked about during that game of pool. At some point our conversation had turned to God. My buddy flat-out asked me if I believed in God. Suddenly it seemed as if this part of my memory was slowed down for me. Mentally I was back in that basement having that conversation and experiencing anew all the emotions that came with it. I could hear the crack of the pool balls and the sound they made when they dropped into the plastic-bottomed pockets. When my friend asked me if I believed in God, my first thought was, *Of course I do.* But when I opened my mouth to answer him, I hesitated.

Have you ever had a rush of thoughts in a split second that would take several minutes to try to explain? You might see a child playing and seconds later you're thinking about flying in an airplane. You try to retrace your thoughts but don't even remember how you got to thinking about flying. That's what happened to me during that game of pool. In the second it took me to open my mouth, my thoughts went from believing in God to flat-out denying any possibility of it.

It had been so long since I had thought about God that I was answering from my old beliefs. All this rushed through my head in a split second. The way I was living my life would not allow for the existence of God. It seemed so silly. Belief in God was only a crutch for the weak, the very people we had just been making fun of. At that moment, without another thought or a care, I decided to deny God. I opened my mouth and said, "No!" In a fraction of time, I made a decision that would determine my destiny. One simple game of pool and one seemingly harmless conversation sealed my fate.

*In one second I went from believing in God to denying Him.*

Seeing the surprised look on my friend's face, I went further. "If there is a God, then how could He allow bad things to happen? If God exists, let Him strike me dead right now!" I held my pool stick boastfully in the air, stuck out my chest and proclaimed again, "Yes, if God is real, then let Him strike me with lightning right now!" I held that position for a moment and then looked back at my friend. "You see," I said, "God's not real." I went back to my game feeling a little uneasy about what had just happened but there was no mistaking that I had willingly made the decision to renounce God.

## TRYING TO PRAY

I came to and found myself lying on the living room floor. I didn't remember blacking out and had no idea how long I had been lying there. I was so remorseful for making that stupid, foolish decision to deny God. The magnitude of my stupidity so overwhelmed me that nothing else mattered. My deepening awareness that I alone was responsible for my plight only made it worse. Feeling my sanity slipping away, I grabbed a blanket, wrapped it around me and started rolling around on the floor like a madman, screaming and biting the blanket. I must have looked like a movie character having a fit in a psychiatric ward. I was ashamed of the decisions I had made, and now I was living with the consequences.

In life we all find ways to avoid consequences. We lie to others or to ourselves. We get drunk or find some way to blame others for what is happening in our lives. My problem was that I was no longer alive. I had no one to blame but me and nowhere to go but down. Even if I walked out the door I would still be in hell. No matter what I tried, I could not get away from the consequences that I had created for myself. My fate was sealed, and there was no turning back.

As I said, I don't know how long I was on the floor. When I finally looked up, I thought about God once again. The moment I did, however, my conscience reminded me that I was getting what I deserved. I tried to pray, but I didn't know what to do. I remember saying just the word, "God." Just as that name rolled off my tongue, I heard a chorus of wild screams. The detachment of demons assigned to me would not allow that kind of chance. My gut reaction was to try again, but they became so angry and so frightening and stirred up so much fear in me that I just closed my mouth and lowered my head. Who was I kidding? It was too late. I had my chance to accept God, but I threw it away. In the name of self-pursuit, I had become my own god. I was the one in control of my eternity and I had put it right into the hands of these creatures. Not only had I wasted my life, but I also had been wrong about everything in the process.

I don't know if you have ever spent time doing something only to find out that you were headed in the wrong direction, but that's what I had done. I had spent my entire life trying to gratify my carnal desires. My life was now over and I was facing eternity in everlasting torment. I now believed in God, but it was too late. You can't possibly imagine how tormenting it is to believe in God and feel like there is no chance for Him to help you. I didn't even know what repentance was, but that is what I tried to do. Even though I didn't think He could hear me, I still wanted to apologize. I wanted to tell God how sorry I was that I had turned my back on Him. I told Him that I now could see how people go to hell.

*Even if I walked out the door I would still be in hell.*

Going to hell had nothing to do with God sending me there. I chose this road. I chose to spit in His face and doom myself to hell. I recognized the feeling. It was the exact same feeling I had when I renounced Him during that game of pool, only intensified a thousandfold. At the time my heart had tried to tell me I was making the wrong decision, but my pride squelched it. My heart even produced the emotions of loss, but I shook them off and continued my game. Had I known I was playing more than pool that day, I would have dropped down on my knees and accepted God right then and there. I wasn't just playing pool. That day in my basement I was playing with my life...and lost.

44

## THE DOG FROM HELL AND THE MONSTERS' DANCE

The emotional agony I was experiencing is beyond description. My mind was barely able to contain the torment. There were moments when I could have let everything fade to black. That's when I had to make a conscious, deliberate decision to hold on. It took every ounce of my strength to keep from slipping into uncontrollable insanity. Even though I felt hopeless and that it was too late for God, it eased my mind a little just to think about Him.

I passed in and out of consciousness. The moments when I was unconscious, I thought about God and what it would have been like to live with Him. As soon as I woke up, however, I heard the onslaught of demons reminding me where I really was. Every time I went somewhere in my thinking, as soon as I came back, they were there. It's like they could tell when I was not aware of them because they tried even harder to reinforce their existence whenever I turned my focus back to them.

I felt like I was on an emotional roller coaster. There were moments when I could endure the mental barrage while others left me screaming and rolling around on the floor like a lunatic. One particular moment when my fear was at a peak, I lifted my head from the floor and found myself face to face with a dog that was in the house. The dog was simply staring at me, but a rush of fear surged through me so strongly that I jumped back from the dog in terror, convinced that it was going to jump on me and rip my flesh to shreds. My mind was already making it real. Already I could feel its teeth digging into me. Of course, that poor dog never did attack me, but as far as I was concerned it had already happened.

After my encounter with the dog, I became aware once more of the people with me. Their faces still had that look of ridicule. When they saw me looking at them, they again asked me if I was okay. This only added to my torment. Okay? Okay?? Of course I wasn't okay, and they knew it! They knew I wasn't okay and they knew I would never be okay! Who were they trying to kid? I wished they would just stop talking to me and leave me alone.

For a time they did stop talking. Then they decided to turn on the television. I didn't know what to expect, but my fears were only confirmed. On the screen were these strange-looking, zombie-like creatures. With a jolt of surprise I realized that I recognized them. We were watching a program that was showing classic videos that at the moment just happened to be running Michael Jackson's *Thriller*. In my childhood I was a huge fan of the *Thriller* video, but now it was completely different. As I watched this "monsters' dance," I just knew they were going to dance right out of the TV and suck me into some deeper part of hell. My "friends" started asking me questions about Michael Jackson. Did I like him? Did I think he was a good dancer? I know now that they were simply trying to get through to me, but at the time I knew they had other intentions. In my twisted, deceived mental state, I took their questions as taunts intended merely to dig the knife of torment in that much deeper.

Have you ever seen a movie or maybe even been in a situation where someone has beaten up someone else and then begins to taunt him or her with silly or obvious questions just for the sake of humiliation? The victor knows he has won and now wants only to shame and humiliate his victim. That's the way I felt about every question I was asked the rest of that night. I felt as though the demons were just messing with my head and rubbing in their victory. They constantly reminded me that I was dead and in hell. They acted like they knew my fate better than I did and were interested in nothing but creating shame, humiliation and fear. As if that wasn't enough, they kept this concept of a "deeper hell" very much in the forefront of my thinking. That concept stuck with me as the primary source of my torment for the next year.

I couldn't watch television, so I just walked away. As I stared out a window into the dark night listening to these demons celebrate their victory, I began to have a few thoughts of my own. I started thinking about God again. All the while the demons kept telling me that there was no hope for me now because I was already dead and God didn't save dead people. I tried to pray again but felt like I was being choked. Once again, accepting what these demons told me, I put the idea out of my head that God could help me. It would be three or four months before I tried to pray again.

Chapter   Four

# FACE TO FACE

⊹

Surprisingly enough, the devil has no creativity of his own. The only tools he has to use against us are those that we give him. This fact was borne out in the next phase of my nightmarish experience, which brought me back to something I had exposed myself to at an earlier age.

The night was progressing slowly with not much interaction between myself and the other people in the room. At some point I found myself back in front of the television. A particular comedy show came on and what I saw and heard added new levels of torment and confusion to my already tortured mind. As I watched the show, I began to realize that the characters were talking about me! I only remember one specific statement. At one point, one of the characters cracked a joke, and I just buried my head in my knees and cringed. Then I heard him say, "I guess he didn't like that one."

Even stranger than hearing myself talked about on TV was the fact that I recognized the characters. Sometime before, I had taken some Ecstasy laced with heroin and gone to see a movie called *Nightbreed*. During the movie the main character had to come to terms with the fact that he had crossed over to death and now had to become a "Nightbreed." I remember thinking, after watching *Nightbreed*, how cool it was that this character would live forever. He was introduced to an underground world of the living dead. At first he fought against who he had become. He tried to run, but the limitations of his new identity would not let him escape.

I now found myself in the very same position. When I saw these same movie creatures on the TV, I immediately "knew" that I had to fully accept that same reality and live the life of a person in hell. Movies had a considerable influence on me at this time in my life. I suppose this is why so much of my experience had to do with movie themes.

## CLUB "HELL"

What happened next was visually the most bizarre occurrence of the evening thus far (if you can believe it!). I thought at first that the appearance of these creatures on this particular show was coincidental, but I quickly discovered that I was terribly wrong. As the show progressed, the creatures, who looked like mutated humans, stopped following the theme of a comedy show and actually turned toward me and began talking directly to me. They looked me straight in the eye and described what was happening as the scene behind them became increasingly dark and hellish looking. In fact, it looked exactly like the same spinning fog I had seen in the car. I even saw the same letters float-ing behind them, spelling out the words *DEATH* and *HELL*.

These living dead "nightbreed" creatures told me that I had become one of them. I was now dead and part of their world. I noticed that they were standing at the entrance of what looked like a club. Just beyond the doors they were guarding was a murky fog. Looking closer, I saw a velvet rope. One of the creatures, an overweight man with octo-pus-like tentacles protruding from his stomach, was playing the role of a bouncer. When he saw me looking at the rope, he reached down and unlocked it. As he did so, I sensed that same horrible, but now familiar, sinking feeling deep in my soul. I could not pull my eyes away. I felt like the gaping hole in my soul led right into the television. At any moment, I knew I was going to be sucked in. Then I heard one of them say, "This is it; here it comes."

I had heard this before and knew exactly what it meant. It was time for my next death. I was paralyzed with fear and could only stare at the television, just waiting to be drawn in and thrust into the next level of hell. Wait! This was too soon! I wasn't ready! This time, however, I did something about it. I closed my eyes, buried my head in the blanket that was still wrapped around me and yelled, "NO!" As soon as I raised my voice I heard scornful laughter. The demons were amused at my reaction. They took great joy in my fear. The more fearful I became, the happier they seemed to be.

## DOCTOR SATAN

I'm not sure when the television went back to a "normal" show, but the next time I looked up the picture had totally changed. The creatures were no longer there; they were replaced by what appeared to be a late-night talk show. I was so relieved to not see those creatures anymore! My relief didn't last long. One guest on the show was dressed in surgical scrubs like a doctor. The host *"I'll be* asked him a question about his profession. His answer froze my heart with chill horror. *waiting."* He said he was waiting for *me!* Then he turned, looked right at me and said, "I'll be waiting." That sinking feeling struck me again so suddenly and so forcefully that I literally jumped over the back of the sofa to escape it.

What did he mean, "I'll be waiting"? Who was he? He didn't look like one of the demonic creatures I had previously seen, yet he seemed just as evil. In fact, he actually seemed more diabolical than any other being I had encountered the entire night. At first I had no idea who he was. I could not stop thinking about him. Gradually, a dawning awareness of his identity awoke in my mind and the fear in my heart multiplied tenfold. No, it couldn't be! My mind wanted to reject what it knew to be true. Now I knew who had said, "I'll be waiting." He was the one who was behind everything that had happened to me all night. *It was Satan himself!* My mind was about to explode with terror! I wanted to jump up, run away and never stop.

Only hours before I would have denied the existence of any kind of afterlife, and now I was trying desperately to figure out how to get away from the devil. His face was ingrained in my mind. I could hear his voice echoing in my ears. I couldn't stay inside anymore; I had to get out. I jumped up, ran through the house, bolted through the kitchen door and started running down the driveway as fast as I could. Even as I ran I knew that I would have to go back. I couldn't escape by running; I was in hell. My only choice was to turn around and face him.

## PRINCE OF DARKNESS

I stopped running, turned around and looked at the house. The effects of the acid were wearing off, but my vision was still distorted. The house looked like the gates of hell. It appeared to be melting but never actually got any lower. I looked down at my feet and had to force myself to take a step. Slowly I walked back to the house. I didn't know what was going to happen, but I knew I had to go. It was as though I was supposed to meet someone I couldn't avoid. No one else was outside, but I knew I wasn't alone. The closer I got to the house, the quieter the demons became. With every step I took, the silence grew deeper. It was so quiet that I actually looked around for the demons that were now so familiar to me. I could still feel them, but they were completely silent.

It was a silence of anticipation. I knew they were watching me closely. As I got about 20 yards away from the house, I heard someone moving. The corner of the garage was shaded by a large tree, creating what looked like a hole in the ground. I stopped walking and just watched. A figure came around the corner and walked toward me. As he entered the light, I immediately knew who he was. There was absolutely no doubt in my mind. It was Satan. I don't want to glorify the devil by any means, but the only way I can describe his appearance is that he looked like a king.

Make no mistake; Satan is *not* a king! He is an imposter and a complete fraud, but I did not know this at the time. He looked like a king and since he seemed to have complete power over me, I accepted him as such.

His presence was heavy. The surrounding demons were still completely quiet, as if paralyzed themselves. They didn't seem to take pleasure in his arrival, but they did seem to give him respect. I can't explain how I understood what was happening; I just did. The demons did not seem familiar with him. I got the feeling that they really didn't know him. Even in the movies, demons usually are presented as Satan's army. The popular notion is that Satan has some organized system of demons that he controls, but that is not what I saw this night. The demons didn't act as if their lord had appeared, but a police officer. They just stood completely still in sullen silence and did absolutely nothing.

Satan had a peculiar look on his face as he approached. He looked like one of the people I was with that night, but there was no mistaking that this was no longer my friend. He walked right up to me and looked deep into my eyes. I now found myself in the most frightening position of the night. *I was standing face to face with the devil!* His presence seemed somehow familiar. For a long time he didn't say anything. He just stared at me, wanting me to fully grasp who he was. Sadistically, he wanted me to experience the full effect of every negative emotion that was surging through my body. He wanted the fear to sink into my very bones. The sense of anticipation was almost unbearable.

## TALKING WITH THE DEVIL

I didn't know whether he was going to usher me into the lower depths of hell or start ripping me apart. He stood there for what seemed like hours before breaking the silence. Finally, he opened his mouth to speak. I watched his lips move but his very first words were not what I expected. He said, "How are you holding up so far?" I was shocked. This confused me more than anything else that had happened so far. Then something even stranger happened. I didn't understand his question at first, but his words were followed by a concept that imprinted itself on my mind. It was like I was hearing two different people. I heard his words with my ears, but in my mind I heard his intention.

*I heard his words with my ears, but in my mind I heard his intention.*

He was speaking to me in two different modes. There was a duality in his nature that I had a hard time adjusting to. His words spoke of being my friend, but with his inner communication he told me that I was his. With his words he assured me that he was going to go through all this with me, but that is not at all how he made me feel. I got the distinctly unpleasant sense that he was telling me what he wanted me to believe, but on the inside was just itching to kill me.

We turned and began walking down the driveway. He put his arm around my waist and suggested that I put my arm around his shoulders. As I reached up, I felt the overwhelming sense that he was going to stab me. I could feel the energy he was projecting as if he was swinging a knife toward my ribs with his other hand. I jumped away from him and shouted, "Don't stab me!" He gave me a confused look and said, "I would never stab you." He didn't try to pull me back to him, but I felt as though he wanted to grab me violently and squeeze me. I kept my distance as we continued our conversation.

He told me that it had been a long time since we had seen each other and how he'd missed talking to me. Internally, the concepts I received from him were not so friendly. He persuaded me to believe that I was one of his family, that the two of us went way back and that we would be together again soon. He impressed on me that I had been his since before time and that after my next death I would again be with him. By this time, he was communicating more internally than with spoken words.

He was very sure of himself. Pride radiated from every inch of his being. It was obvious he took joy in his own words and in hearing himself talk. He was like a king who had let his power go to his head. The duality of his communication was subtly deceitful. As the conversation progressed, he continued to say one thing and speak to me internally something completely different. We stood outside face to face for most of the conversation. He never let me out of his sight. The main concept that he wanted me to walk away with was that I *belonged* to him.


## A MAN'S GOT TO DO WHAT A MAN'S GOT TO DO.

Just when I thought the conversation was over, he gave me a kind of commission. The following is a synopsis of what he said to me. Some statements are exact and some are based on my best recollection.

Satan said to me:

"You have brought yourself to this place. You are experiencing what you are because of decisions that you made. It's time for you to take responsibility for

56

your death. It's time for you to accept your eternity as it now is. There is no way for you to get out of what you have created for yourself. From now on, you no longer have anyone you can turn to. You no longer have anything. I'm trying to help you out. I'm trying to help you through this. It won't be easy, but I'll be here with you. I'll be the one that is with you every step of the way. You can never get away from me."

The very last thing he said to me was, "A man's got to do what a man's got to do." With that, he turned and walked away.

That statement would be a source of torment for me for months. It was the nail in the coffin. I fell down in the driveway and stared at the sky. I knew what I had to do. I knew that I was dead and had to spend eternity in hell. I had created this situation and now I had to "live" with it. My sins had placed me here. Since there was no one else to take that burden, I carried it all by myself. I had passed into a sick realm of guilt and punishment from which I would never escape. This terrifying state of affairs was my eternity and, even worse, I knew it was going to *get* worse. Before I had "died," I had always loved movies, particularly horror films. Now I was the "star" of my own horror story, playing the lead role as the dead man. But this was no movie. I wouldn't be walking out at the end and going home. I *was* "home" and I would be there forever.

The demons made sure I understood my situation in this new "reality." Since I was in hell by my own doing, I had to accept responsibility. I decided that since I hadn't done the right thing while I was alive, I would do the right thing while I was in this state of existence. Once again the statement, "A man's got to do what a man's got to do," came to my mind. It was like a mental trigger. Any time I started feeling sorry for myself, that statement flashed into my mind, ever deepening the sense of guilt and shame that weighed me down.

From then on guilt, shame and fear dominated my emotions. No longer would I laugh, experience joy, or have the sense of living in a free country. No matter what I did, the phrase "A man's got to do what a man's got to do" would remind me of where I was, how I'd gotten there, and the responsibility that came with it. Of course, it was all deception, but I didn't know it. This was the demons' way of keeping me in the dark and making sure I "played the game."

# Chapter Five

# JESUS AT THE
# CROSSROADS

Without exception, every one of us at some point comes to a crossroads in life. Eventually we all face a decision of one kind or another where the outcome will determine the course of our entire future. It may be a choice between investing in a risky but potentially lucrative business venture or playing it safe and holding on to our money. It may involve deciding which course of treatment to pursue after a cancer diagnosis. It may deal with choosing a college or deciding which profession to pursue. Sometimes decisions that seem minor at the time prove later to have serious ramifications. That's what I discovered about my decision to deny God during that game of pool. That decision came back to haunt me in a big way.

One crossroads we all must face is the decision of what to do with regard to God's claim on our lives. The Bible presents us with two kingdoms: God's kingdom of light and life and Satan's so-called "kingdom" of darkness and death. I say "so-called" because Satan is *not* a king, even though he likes to fancy himself as such. He is an imposter, a fraud, a liar and the author of lies. The choice the Bible offers us is clear: Choose God and choose life or choose Satan and choose death.

Satan may be a liar and a fraud, but that doesn't mean he cannot exert influence in our lives. He is also crafty, cunning and clever, a master deceiver. During my nightmarish encounter with the demonic world, even including my face-to-face meeting with the devil, I could have chosen at any time to end it by simply refusing to accept what I was being told. His deceptions were so artful and my defenses so weakened that I fell right into his lies. I was at a crossroads and didn't even know it.

Although such encounters are rare, I am neither the first nor the only person to meet Satan face to face at a crossroads, and I probably won't be the last. Even Jesus, the Son of God, had a face-off with Satan. The outcome of that encounter set the course for the rest of Jesus' life and ministry. Even Jesus had to face His crossroads, and His preparation for that encounter began from the moment He was born in that stable in Bethlehem.

## JESUS HAD TO PREPARE FOR HIS CROSSROADS

Luke 2:40 says of Jesus, *"And the child grew, and waxed strong in spirit, filled with wisdom: and the grace of God was upon him."*

This scripture indicates that Jesus grew in the wisdom of God. The fact that He had to *grow* in God's wisdom means that even though He was the Son of God, He was not born with the full wisdom of God. Like every other human child, Jesus had to grow in wisdom, faith and knowledge. He didn't know everything God knew. He didn't come out of the womb healing people and walking on water. Yes, the Holy Spirit was in Him and yes, He was the Son of God, but as Luke indicated, even Jesus had to grow in God. He had to prepare for what lay ahead.

Later, at the very beginning of His public ministry, Jesus revealed His mission as He understood it. Again, Luke provided the details:

*And he came to Nazareth, where he had been brought up: and, as his custom was, he went into the synagogue on the sabbath day, and stood up for to read. And there was delivered unto him the book of the prophet Esaias. And when he had opened the book, he found the place where it was written, The Spirit of the Lord is upon me, because he hath anointed me to preach the gospel to the poor; he hath sent me to heal the brokenhearted, to preach deliverance to the captives, and recovering of sight to the blind, to set at liberty them that are bruised, To preach the acceptable year of the Lord. And he closed the book, and he gave it again to the minister, and sat down. And the eyes of all them that were in the synagogue were fastened on him. And he began to say unto them, This day is this scripture fulfilled in your ears* (Luke 4:16-21).

That day in the synagogue when Jesus announced that He was the Messiah, Luke said that He flipped to a passage in Isaiah and read from it. Let's take a little journey together. Given what we have already established about Jesus growing in God, can't you see Jesus as a young boy poring over the Scriptures just as every young Hebrew male did? He knew about the coming of the Messiah and knew what the Messiah would accomplish. Can't you see Him reading in Isaiah 52 and 53 about the suffering the Messiah would have to endure in order to complete God's plan of salvation? Jesus' understanding of these passages is evident in the Garden of Gethsemane when Jesus prays to His Father to *"let this cup pass from me"* (Matthew 26:39).

*By the time He was 12, Jesus knew His identity and mission.*

In this instance, *"cup"* means "lot in life"; His "cup" of suffering. Jesus was asking His Father if there was any other way to accomplish the salvation of humanity than by His suffering and death. Can you see Jesus thinking back to all those times He had read the Scriptures about the suffering of the Messiah? Early on in His life, Jesus connected with the truth that He was the Messiah and that all those Scriptures referred to Him. According to Luke, by the time Jesus was 12 years old, He already knew who He was and what He was supposed to do (see Luke 2:42-49). In the garden, just hours before His crucifixion, He remembered those Scriptures again. In the end, of course, He obeyed the will of His Father and willingly faced the pain and suffering and humiliation of the cross so that people like you and me could be brought into relationship with God.

Gethsemane was a crossroads for Jesus. But it was not His first. Somewhere between the time He was a child waxing strong in spirit, filled with wisdom and the grace of God, and the day He announced His mission in the Nazarene synagogue, Jesus faced another crossroads—a point of decision where He had to choose what kind of Messiah He was going to be. This was more than just a mental or intellectual exercise, however, because through it all Jesus faced off with an adversary that sought at every juncture to turn Him from the path set out by His Father. At this critical crossroads, Jesus went face to face with the devil.

Let's let Luke tell the story.

*And Jesus being full of the Holy Ghost returned from Jordan, and was led by the Spirit into the wilderness, being forty days tempted of the devil. And in those days he did eat nothing: and when they were ended, he afterward hungered. And the devil said unto him, If thou be the Son of God, command this stone that it be made bread. And Jesus answered him, saying, It is written, That man shall not live by bread alone, but by every word of God. And the devil, taking him up into an high mountain, showed unto him all the kingdoms of the world in a moment of time. And the devil said unto him, All this power will I give thee, and the glory of them: for that is delivered unto me; and to whomsoever I will I give it. If thou therefore wilt worship me, all shall be thine. And Jesus answered and said unto him, Get thee behind me, Satan: for it is written, Thou shalt worship the Lord thy God, and him only shalt thou serve. And he brought him to Jerusalem, and set him on a pinnacle of the temple,*

63

*and said unto him, If thou be the Son of God, cast thyself down from hence: for it is written, He shall give his angels charge over thee, to keep thee: and in their hands they shall bear thee up, lest at any time thou dash thy foot against a stone. And Jesus answering said unto him, It is said, Thou shalt not tempt the Lord thy God. And when the devil had ended all the temptation, he departed from him for a season* (Luke 4:1-13).

According to Luke, the first thing Jesus did after John the Baptist baptized Him in the Jordan River was go into the wilderness under the leading of the Holy Spirit, where He was *"tempted of the devil."* Both Matthew and Luke record a detailed account of this event and both indicate that Jesus was subjected to three specific temptations, all of which concern His identity and the nature of His mission on earth.

The accounts are specific; these were not simply mental battles that Jesus fought. Satan appeared to Him in visible, tangible form and revealed his nature as a master tempter.

In the first temptation, Satan tried to play on the fact of Jesus' physical hunger. After 40 days without food, of course Jesus was hungry. Satan said, "If You're the Son of God, turn this stone to bread and feed yourself." Satan was not interested in satisfying Jesus' hunger, so what trick was he trying to pull? What was his real reason for asking Jesus to turn stones to bread? Was he testing Jesus to see if He could really do it? No. Satan knew who Jesus was and was fully aware of His power. Look at the nature of Satan's question: *"If thou be the Son of God...."* This was really a taunt from the devil to provoke Jesus into proving His identity. In response, Jesus quoted scripture to the effect that there is more to life than simply satisfying physical hunger and that true life comes not from bread but from the Word of God.

Rebuffed on that front, Satan tried a different tack. Taking Jesus to a *"high mountain,"* the devil showed Him all the kingdoms of the world and promised to give them to Him if Jesus would only bow and worship him. This was a challenge to Jesus to reveal Himself as King of kings earlier than God planned and by a route that would allow Him to avoid the cross. Like every other scenario the devil spins, it was a lie and Jesus saw right through it. Again, He quoted scripture that stated plainly that God and God *alone* was to be worshiped.

Twice defeated, the devil made a final attempt. He took Jesus to Jerusalem and placed Him on a pinnacle of the temple, one of the highest points on the structure. Challenging Jesus to jump from the pinnacle, Satan this time quoted (and misused) scripture himself (he's a sly weasel, isn't he!), a promise from the Psalms that God would send angels to lift Jesus up and keep Him from falling. In this instance, the devil was tempting Jesus to reveal His identity through His own works and sensational signs rather than the way God had laid out for Him. Jesus responded with more scripture: a prohibition against subjecting God to a foolish and presumptuous test.

That is exactly the same place where we find ourselves. Whenever we seek to establish our own identity on our own outside of God's leading us, we are limited to our own strength. Instead of trusting God and following Him, we jump ahead of Him, thinking that we know best. I know I have found myself there many times and I'm sure you have too.

Had Jesus surrendered to any of these temptations, He would have become a different kind of Messiah than the one His Father sent Him to be, which means that, in truth, He would have been no Messiah at all because He would have stood in disobedience to His Father. Jesus stood firm, however, and defeated Satan, who then departed from Jesus *"for a season."* This means that Jesus' temptations were not over.

*We resist the devil, not attack him!*

How are we supposed to deal with the devil? Listen to James 4:7: *"Submit yourselves therefore to God. Resist the devil, and he will flee from you."* The word *resist* here doesn't mean to attack; it simply means to guard ourselves in defense. It's interesting to note that the Bible doesn't tell us to attack the devil but simply to resist him and he will leave. This sheds a whole new light on the concept of "aggressive spiritual warfare"!

Like all of us, Jesus had to deal with temptation all the way up to His death. Unlike all of us, however, He never gave in and never sinned. Hebrews 4:15 affirms this: *"For we have not an high priest which cannot be touched with the feeling of our infirmities; but was in all points tempted like as we are, yet without sin."*

## WAS IT REAL?

There is one other interesting aspect to this story that I want to look at, an aspect that is almost always overlooked. Luke said in verse 5 that the devil *took* Jesus to a *"high mountain"* and in verse 9 that he *brought* Jesus to Jerusalem and *put* Him on a pinnacle of the temple. Are we to read this literally? Did Satan actually, physically, do these things with Jesus? How is that possible? We could say that God granted the devil the ability to do this, but there is no mention of that in the text. Someone might suggest that Jesus' hunger caused Him to hallucinate, but that's not completely accurate either. The Bible says the devil *took* Jesus to these places. Does the devil have that kind of power? Can he cause us to see whatever he wants us to see?

The original language indicates that the word *took* reveals a willingness of the part of the one being taken. Jesus went willingly because the devil could not have taken Him anywhere against His will. The question is, did they actually *go* anywhere? How was Jesus able to see the holy city and all the kingdoms of the world that the devil showed him from that mountain? Was Jesus actually in these places or were they hallucinations? Did the devil really take him to those physical locations or did he somehow create some kind of illusion that Jesus would see these things?

I do not claim to know the correct answer, but it seems apparent from Jesus' response that these visions were real to *Him*. He did not say, "What are you talking about? We're in the middle of the desert, not on top of the temple in Jerusalem!" or "What mountain? I can't see any kingdoms from this desolate place!" Nowhere in the text is there the slightest hint that Jesus questioned the validity either of what He saw or of the devil's offers.

So again we come to the question, does the devil have the power to deceive us and create illusions for us that can change the course of our lives? I hope you see the connection between this question, Jesus' temptation experience in the wilderness and my own encounter with the devil on that dark and dreadful night.

Yes, the devil does have the power to deceive us and create illusions to send us down the wrong path, but *only if we allow him to.* The choice is always ours. At His crossroads Jesus chose not to be deceived and not to believe the devil's illusions and therefore won the victory. At my crossroads, I chose to believe the lies the devil told me and spent the next year in a living hell on earth.

# Chapter Six

# MAKING A DEAL
# WITH THE DEVIL

—•— ⁂ —•—

Faced with a choice between believing Satan's lies or rejecting them and seeking another path, I chose the lies. Of course, I was being deceived big-time and was given only one side of the story (Satan's side), and I had no other spiritual reference point from my own life to draw on. Considering these factors, how could I have chosen otherwise? Yet, the choice was mine. I alone bear the responsibility for what happened. When the lies came, telling me that I was dead and in hell, I didn't even question them; I simply gave in.

Once I fully surrendered to my new "reality," the effect was immediate. Paranoia became my new norm. I felt like the star attraction in a diabolic three-ring circus with the entire mob of demons watching me continually and waiting to ridicule and pick apart every move I made. My every thought and decision was driven by consideration for what these demons would think about me.

*Demons have no morals, integrity or character.*

They were my audience, and like any good actor I catered to the desires of my audience.

The primary desire of my particular audience was that I live in fear and mental torment until I had no mental capacity left. This is exactly how Satan and demons work. They constantly try to wear us down. They wait until we are at our weakest and then, like the spineless creatures they are, they attack. Demons have no morals, integrity or character. They will stop at nothing to sway us to believe what they want us to believe. The more I listened to them, the more heinous their methods and thoughts and accusations became.

Think about the most horrific acts of torture or murder that you have ever heard of. Even the very worst of those acts pale in comparison to the obscenities of thought and behavior that demonic creatures can conceive. Their minds are thoroughly twisted and absolutely corrupt.

These detestable creatures wanted to make me suffer unremitting mental anguish and keep my mind consumed with how horrible they were going to make my existence. They wanted my thoughts to be overwhelmed with visions of all the deaths I was going to have to endure. Never for a single moment did they let me forget that my eternal destiny was to experience death again and again. Hindus believe in reincarnation, a virtually endless cycle of death and rebirth that hopefully will end some day when the soul is released into the nothingness of nirvana. As horrible as that prospect seems, mine was even worse. I faced an endless cycle of deaths with no rebirths in between and no hope of ever escaping.

## COPING WITH HELL

During the whole time Satan was in my presence, the horde of demons had remained absolutely quiet. As soon as the devil departed, however, they immediately resumed their mind-numbing chatter and didn't stop for months.

I walked back into the house with a new look on life, or should I say, death. Now that I had come to terms with my new reality, I actually began thinking of ways to cope with being in hell. The phrase, "A man's got to do what a man's got to do," kept swimming through my head. It served only to further deepen the sense of responsibility I felt for where my life had led me. I looked around the house with new eyes. Words cannot describe what it feels like to have to accept that you will be in hell forever. I sat on the floor and buried my head in my hands and wept. A sense of sorrow and utter hopelessness flooded every inch of my being and settled deep into my spirit.

My shame, guilt and confusion mounted to the point where I sank into deep depression. Every second that passed felt like an eternity. I now understand why the Bible says there will be weeping and gnashing of teeth for those who spend eternity in hell. The emptiness in my heart that felt like a black hole returned, and now it was even darker than before. There was a void in the middle of my chest that could not be filled. It was a familiar sensation because I had felt it all my life. I had tried to fill it with drugs, sex and other immoral behavior, but it never went away. Now that I was dead, I knew that the void in my chest would always be there, gnawing at me like a festering and unclosed wound. I now knew also that only God could fill that void, but I had rejected God and it was too late for me.

That set me to thinking about Jesus and how I had rejected Him. I would have expected that going to hell would make me mad at Jesus, but it only made me want Him even more. For me, it took going to hell to find out the truth about God. I wanted desperately to talk to Him, but I also understood that He could not come where I was. I finally recognized what Jesus had done for me...and I had missed it. That revelation came as the worst blow of all. Things could have been different, but now I was in hell and it was all my fault. I couldn't even talk to Jesus to tell Him how sorry I was. I don't know if you have ever lost someone and just wanted one last chance to talk to him or her, but that is how I felt.

*Going to hell only made me want Jesus more.*

I was so frustrated because everything around me looked like my old life, but I knew it wasn't. The familiarity of my surroundings only reinforced in my mind the magnitude of what I had lost. Everywhere I looked I was reminded of things I would never experience again. I thought about how I would never talk to my friends again. Thoughts of my family surfaced again, especially of my mom, and thinking of her only made me cry harder. All that was gone forever. My fate had been determined. My soul had faced judgment and come up wanting. Every moment was like hardening concrete cementing into my consciousness the reality of my new state of existence.

By this time the sun had started to come up. I looked outside and saw a blood-red sky. It was a fitting image for the massacre that had occurred during the night. Turning away from the window I noticed that the television was still on. The demon that resembled my female friend had fallen asleep on the floor in front of the TV. Just as my eyes passed over her, she raised her head and in a ridiculing tone asked, "What is this?" At first I thought she was asking me what was on TV, but I quickly determined that her question was a taunt. I became furious when I realized that all she wanted to do was remind me where I was. She was not talking about the television but about my new existence. I lowered my head, turned away and whispered, "This is hell." She laid her head back down as if to signal to me that I was correct.

I went into a bedroom and lay down on the bed, and as I lay there I heard a train in the background. I focused on the rumble of the train in an effort to drown out even for just a few minutes the constant barrage of demonic voices that I knew would never leave me. For the next year, every time I heard a train, the emotions I experienced that night came rushing back like a flood. Looking back, I can see now how several triggers were created in my night—triggers the demons used to make sure I would not forget where I was: dead and hopelessly lost in hell.

## PLAYING DEAD

What happened next still amazes me to this day. I don't remember how long I lay on that bed, but I remember very well the conclusion I came to while lying there. I concluded that since I was dead, I needed to go through the stages a body goes through when it dies. I reasoned that I was still in a realm that looked like my old life because I was still in my body. Getting rid of my body would "free" me to move to the next level of hell. Since it was coming anyway, I thought that perhaps I was the one to determine when I went. If so, that would give me at least a tiny bit of control over my situation.

*The demonic voices told me I could pretend to be dead.*

In short, I believed that I needed to "play dead." Once again fear and dread flooded my body as I lay there and took myself mentally through the process. At first I tried to stop breathing on my own but with no success. While I was still trying to figure out how I could make my body appear dead, the demonic voices told me that I could just lie there and pretend to be dead. I accepted this and in my thoughts moved to the next phase.

Eventually, I reasoned, people would come in and find me dead. They would call an ambulance and I would be taken to a morgue. I was so thoroughly convinced of the reality of my situation that I actually came to believe that I would have to lie perfectly still on the coroner's table while he performed an autopsy on me. Since I was dead, I knew I could not get around this sequence of events. I tried to imagine what it would feel like to have that scalpel slice my body open and the coroner's hands moving around in my body cavity and removing my organs.

The image suddenly became so real to me that I jumped off the bed. I was shivering in fear, but that same familiar phrase flashed into my mind again: "A man's got to do what a man's got to do." I stretched back out on the bed and didn't move again.

Some time later, I heard movement from the next room. The voices of my "copied" friends grew louder as they got closer to where I lay. When they walked into the room, they were talking about me, asking each other if they thought I was okay and remarking about how crazy I had acted last night. This came across to me as a personal attack. I heard every word they said but forced myself to endure my accepted fate. No matter what they said, I remained completely still.

After a little discussion among themselves, my "friends" decided to try to wake me up. I kept my eyes shut and didn't move a muscle. They called my name several times, growing louder and louder when I failed to respond. Finally, when they realized that I was not going to wake up, they decided to pick me up. I felt their hands slide under my arms and pull me toward the edge of the bed. My mind was racing. I still believed I was on my way to the morgue, but a second later I heard a voice say, "Here it comes." I knew what that meant! They weren't trying to wake me up; they were trying to drag me into the next level of hell! Inside I was screaming, but externally I submitted my body to my inescapable future.

## CHOOSING THE LIE

They dragged me out of the room, down the hall and out the door onto the driveway, where they started shaking me, trying to wake me up. I relaxed my muscles even more and let my captors continue to act out what they seemed to be having so much fun doing. At some point, my arms were in so much pain that I had to do something to ease the discomfort. I moved my shoulders and shifted my head a little to the left, and when I did, the people dragging me became more determined than ever to wake me.

Finally, I lifted my head, opened my eyes and stood on my feet. My "friends" immediately began questioning me. They asked me what I was doing, which felt to me like only another attempt to inflict more mental torture. Although everything they said had a perfectly innocent face value meaning, to my mind it also had a second, more sinister meaning intended to solidify even more in my thinking the reality of my new existence.

At some point, one of them asked me who I thought he was. I looked at him and said, "You are death." The expression on that face I knew so well switched suddenly from fear to anger. He jumped back from me and started yelling. I didn't even hear what he said; I simply closed up and tuned him out. This must have enraged him even more because he began pushing me. He kept yelling at me, telling me to listen to him. Finally, I looked at him. He wanted me to stop saying that I was dead and to stop calling him "death." He said that he was going to get in trouble and that I shouldn't say those things anymore.

From this conversation I adopted yet another belief: I now knew that before I would find myself on a coroner's table, I would first have to live out this illusion of life. This was my first phase of hell. I had to act the part of my old self and interact with demons that looked like people. With this new scenario in mind, I agreed to stop calling my screaming friend "death" and accepted the seeming reality that was presented to me. I was now going to have to live in my own personal hell. I was going to have to live a lie.

I walked down the driveway in a daze. After being convinced I was going to be buried alive, I now found myself walking in the street trying to figure out what I was going to do next. I started ask- *This was my* ing myself questions. *Am I supposed to just act like nothing ever happened?* *first phase* *Should I get a gun and shoot myself so I can pass to my next level of hell? Maybe I* *of hell.* *should just go out in the woods and wait until I starve.* My thoughts became more and more morbid.

Somehow I stumbled my way back into my house. I went into my room, sank into my bed, pulled the covers over my head and thought of nothing but my upcoming series of deaths. I imagined my flesh being torn from my bones and spread around in hell. I envisioned thousands of demons chewing on my dismembered body until there was nothing but bones left, then crushing my bones into powder and drinking it. Thoughts of what lay ahead for me left me paralyzed with fear. Just as these devils devoured every last morsel of my body, my body would reform and my consciousness return, only for me to experience the whole horrible scene all over again. I imagined myself being sucked into the engine of a car, ground to pieces in its inner workings and spit out the exhaust. I had visions of hooks flying in from nowhere and tearing my body apart. I saw myself mutilated in car crashes, only to be revived time and time again for another excruciating death. The types of deaths I foresaw for myself were endless. Over the next few months, I would have several spells where I would freeze up and think of nothing but new ways to die.

Finally, over 48 hours after this living nightmare began, I fell asleep. Sleep brought no relief, however, because my dreams were actually worse than my waking thoughts. In my dreams, I talked with demons about what they were going to do to me. My mind was completely open to anything they told me, and they took full advantage of it. Believe it or not, but this kind of torment went on for months. I would wake up every morning and go about my day living the lie that I had accepted back in that driveway.

## LET'S MAKE A DEAL

About a week later, I was watching television and was reminded of a commercial I had seen on that fateful night that gave a phone number for a call that could change everything. As I watched this new commercial, I vaguely remembered the original one and suddenly had the sense that Satan was again talking to me. This was the first time that I had felt him since I talked to him that night. I somehow knew that the phone number was a direct line to Satan and that if I called it, all of this could stop.

For several long minutes I tried desperately and unsuccessfully to remember the phone number. Finally, however, it came to me and I picked up the phone and dialed. All I heard was a recording that said the number had been disconnected. I hung up the phone in despair as my audience of demons burst out in laughter. They thought it was so humorous that I would even attempt something so stupid. They said that I had had my chance to call that night, but I threw it away.

After a few weeks, I actually began to get used to my new existence. It's amazing what we allow to become "normal" in our lives. You may feel that you could never get used to something as extreme as my situation, but what in your life has become "normal" for you that you never believed would? What have you accepted in your life that is really nothing but death to you? My experience was perhaps more extreme than most, but the same principles apply to any situation. There may be something in your life that you know is wrong, but you have come to accept it nevertheless. To me, everyone was a devil. Every conversation I had with anyone was part of this big game that I was in. Nothing was real to me. I didn't understand why, but I knew I had to just keep playing the game. Since all this was my responsibility, I was committed to seeing it through to the end. After all, "a man's got to do what a man's got to do."

*I knew I had to just keep playing the game.*

Before long, I decided to make the best of this version of a life. I had come to terms with my new existence and actually found a way to live with the voices that I still heard constantly. Now I came up with a plan that I thought would bring me some relief. I had seen people make deals with the devil in movies and decided to give it a try for myself. One day I called out for him and felt that he responded. When he arrived, everything felt the same as it did that first night we talked. His whole demeanor was different from that of the demons. He wasn't frantic like they were but exuded a self-confident air that bordered on arrogance.

I told Satan that I wanted to make a deal. Sensing that he was open to the idea, I presented my terms. I told him that I would go with him at the end of this altered life if he would just let me live this life out as my own. I also told him that I knew I was living a lie, but I would rather have that than have to experience the same things I had been experiencing. I knew that I was dead, but I so missed my old life that I was willing to have a fake relationship with demons than have to walk around in hell. Finally, I asked him to leave me alone for the rest of this life. Surprisingly enough, I felt like he agreed.

For a few days, I actually had some relief. I could still sense the host of devils, but they seemed to be quieter. Looking back, I realize now that the relief I experienced came from my decision to try to live a normal life. I soon found out for myself that the devil is a liar. He didn't keep his end of the bargain. Had I read the Bible before, I would have known that truth already. All of hell was still trying to keep me in the overwhelmed frame of mind I had been in, but it somehow didn't feel as strong as before. Even though I felt better, I told myself that I was just now becoming familiar with my new reality and not to forget where I was ultimately headed.

Once I made the decision to keep my end of the bargain I had made with the devil, I felt a strange sense of empowerment. Since I was willing to hold up my end, I thought I was entitled at least to try to experience what I had asked for. Even though the devil wasn't keeping his word, I felt qualified to live somewhat normally, at least for this temporary life. After I started feeling this new sense of freedom, several incidents occurred that almost caused me to give up. When I say "give up," I mean attempted suicide.

The first instance came while I was in the car with one of my closest friends. We were talking about the night this whole thing first started. This was the first time that I had spoken about that night with anyone. It was also the longest conversation I had had with anyone since then. Every other attempt at conversation had ended with me closing my mouth, realizing that it was futile to have a conversation with a demon. Until this point, no matter what the topic, every conversation reminded me of my future in hell.

For some reason, this conversation was different. We started out talking about music and some of our favorite bands. Just when I was feeling as close to normal as I had since that night, he asked me if I had gotten over it. My bubble burst. How could I be so stupid as to think that I could have a real conversation with a devil? As soon as he asked that question, this conversation took the same turn as the previous ones did.

In response to his question I just scoffed. I told him that he knew the truth. He knew that I was dead and I asked him why he would even make fun of me like that. He said he wasn't making fun of me and that he just wanted to help. I scoffed again because I still believed that I was speaking with a demon. I again shut my mouth and drew within myself. He kept on talking. He said he thought I might need mental help and wanted to check me in at a mental institution. He suggested that I might never get over this without help. He said he didn't know what to do, but he could take me to someone who did.

Immediately I saw myself locked up in an institution, drugged up and experiencing even deeper throes of torment. I turned him down.

## ATTACKED BY THE DEVIL

That night as I went to bed I had extremely strong visions of multiple deaths. I also had a terrifying and vivid dream in which I was lying on my sofa watching television. I looked over to my right and noticed a body lying there with its back to me. It felt strangely familiar. I recognized who it was by the presence that surrounded him. It was Satan. I began talking to him, but he just lay there and made no response. I told him to sit up and look at me, that I was angry with him for not keeping his part of our deal. No matter how I pleaded and demanded, he just lay there and said nothing.

Finally, he sat up, looked at me and agreed to talk to me. He said, "Normally I wouldn't do this, but I can tell you are not going to give up."

I pleaded with him to let me out of hell and let me go back to my old life. I didn't think about logistics; I just wanted to go back. I told him that I had learned my lesson and didn't want to be there anymore.

He just looked at me and said, "It's too late, Clint; there is no way you can go back. I will be with you and stay with you until the end of time. You are mine, and that's all there is to it."

With that, he lay back down. That was the last time I would speak face to face with the devil.

As soon as he lay down, I woke up to a crushing sensation like someone was sitting on my back. My room was darker than normal and I heard what sounded like death metal music in the background. I was lying on my stomach with my arms up under my pillow. I tried to pull my arms out but could not. Something was forcing me down on my bed, and I could feel hands on my feet trying to pull me off my bed. I tried to scream but couldn't. Even though I wasn't moving, I felt the strange sensation of being pulled downward toward hell. Finally, I managed to shake my head. As soon as I did, my mouth opened and I screamed, "NO!" The moment I screamed, the crushing and falling sensations left and I was alone on my bed. That was the first and only time that I was physically attacked.

## A STEP IN THE RIGHT DIRECTION

I was half asleep when I was attacked but awake enough to know that it was real. I turned on the lights and sat up in bed so scared that I didn't sleep the rest of the night. Along with my fear I now felt a new emotion: anger. In my dream I was angry at the devil, not so much in a fighting sense as in a sense of justice. For the first time I felt that what he was doing wasn't right. It was wrong for him to torment me like this. After everything else I had been through, this feeling confused me, but it also brought a sense of change into my soul.

I went into the living room and turned on the television to the Christian station. I was completely shocked at what happened. Up until this point, every television show and almost every commercial I had seen reminded me that I was in hell. This show was different. I didn't really understand what the preacher was talking about, but his words somehow made me able to rest. For the first time in a couple of months, I actually had a few minutes where I forgot that I was dead. This man said things that made me feel alive. In my mind I was still convinced that I was dead and in hell, but there were brief moments where I felt something I had never felt before—something good.

Later I learned that this man was a very popular TV evangelist who had been taken off the air for fraud, but I didn't see that in him. In recent years since then, I have seen his show again and all he talks about is money, but that's not what I heard when I first began watching him. I don't even really remember what he said; I just know how I felt. Besides, I didn't pay attention to the money talk. All I focused on was when he mentioned God. I was so amazed by how this made me feel that I became a Christian TV "junkie." It wasn't necessarily because the shows were all that good but because I liked the way they made me feel.

Today I find it absolutely amazing that at the devil's second strongest attack in my life, God was there to point me to a show that could help me even though I was still lost. Not only was I lost, I still predominantly believed that I was dead and in hell. The concrete was beginning to crack, however, just a little. I had just taken my first step in the right direction, a direction that would eventually lead me out of the darkness of lies and death and into the brilliant light of truth and life.

# Chapter Seven

# FROM DARKNESS TO LIGHT

s the weeks wore on, the demons grew quieter and quieter. I still had moments where I felt that I would walk
around a corner and run into a manifested demon that
would suck me into hell, but those moments were growing
farther and farther apart. Even though I still predominantly
believed that I was dead, my sense of peace was stronger
and continued to grow day by day. Deep inside I was still
convinced that I would end up in hell, but something in me
was changing. The demons kept telling me that I was about
to get run over or that some lunatic was going to run into the
house and kill me, but even those threats seemed less real.

An interesting thing happened to me one day that forever shaped my view of the devil. I later found it to be true in

85

the Bible, but I first realized it through experience. I was walking down the hall one day and heard a voice tell me that a demon was waiting around the corner for me. When I turned the corner, nothing was there. At that moment a question arose in my heart. *What about all the other times when I heard something like that but it never happened?* Not a single thing that the voices had told me had ever come true. I thought back to the night all this began and realized that aside from a few instances with the television, most of what had happened to me could be explained.

I began thinking, *Maybe I'm not dead.* I reconsidered that night and the people I was with and what might really have happened. The thought occurred to me that perhaps I had gone through some kind of supernatural experience, that I really had heard the demons and talked with Satan but had not really died. Somehow in some way I had connected to the spiritual realm. I knew that I had encountered real demons. Was it possible that they were lying to me? Had they tricked me into believing that I had died and gone to hell? Was I so vulnerable that night that I was open to believe anything the devil told me?

These thoughts and questions rolled around in my head for days. I would have moments of thinking that I was really alive and then I would hear something or smell something (those implanted triggers) and revert back to thinking that I was dead.

Now, about five months into this nightmare, I was finally starting to see a different reality. For so long I had been consumed with death, but now I had moments of life, real life, again. I was excited yet confused at the same time.

## A GLIMMER OF LIGHT

There was one particular morning when my questioning came to fruition. My challenging of the demons finally paid off. As I was waiting for the water to warm up, I asked myself a simple question. "What about God?" My awareness turned inward to something I had never experienced before. I looked into my soul and saw massive darkness. Once again I felt suspended over that "black hole" of my soul, but this time something was different; I could see a very faint glimmer of light. Immediately my attention was completely fixed on this oh-so-tiny source of light that was like a single star in an otherwise totally dark universe. For the first time in my life, I felt hope. Such a feeling was foreign to me. I was so used to having my hopes dashed that I naturally expected this to go away too. But it didn't.

*Nothing could quench that little light.*

Strong emotions of fear rose up in me almost immediately, but focusing on that light source made the fear endurable and somehow less fearful. Even as tiny as that light was, nothing that came up in my thinking could quench it, no matter how negative or fearful. From this point on my life took a turn. I still believed most of the time that I was dead, but I also now began to believe that somehow God could still help me. With little Christian influence in my background and no prior knowledge of heaven and hell, I didn't know that once you go to hell you can't come back. I had previously believed this from my own experience, but now I actually had hope that God could somehow help.

At first I thought that He could just make this lie of a life better, but slowly I began to think that he could *erase* the lie.

I actually began to have moments when I thought I might even be able to go to heaven. I had no idea what to do, so I just kept watching Christian television. I heard one preacher talking about something I had never understood before: receiving salvation. Immediately I remembered the moment on that night months before when I understood what Jesus had done on the cross. When the TV preacher said something about going to heaven, I was all ears. At the end of his sermon, he offered a chance for people to accept Christ and go to heaven. I was absolutely amazed. I prayed the prayer he suggested and felt wonderful!

In the months since my nightmare had begun, this was the longest I had gone without a thought of being dead. Those thoughts did return, but now they had lost their sting. I was reminded of a poem by John Donne that I had read in high school:

*Death be not proud, though some have called thee*

*Mighty and dreadfull, for, thou art not soe,*

*For, those, whom thou think'st, thou dost overthrow,*

*Die not, poore death, nor yet canst thou kill mee.*

*From rest and sleepe, which but thy pictures bee,*

*Much pleasure, then from thee much more must flow,*

*And soonest our best men with thee doe goe,*

*Rest of their bones, and soules deliverie.*

*Thou art slave to Fate, Chance, kings, and desperate men,*

*And dost with poyson, warre, and sicknesse dwell,*

*And poppie, or charmes can make us sleepe as well,*

*And better then thy stroake; why swell'st thou then?*

*One short sleepe past, wee wake eternally,*

*And death shall be no more; death, thou shalt die.*

I had committed this poem to memory never understanding what it really meant. The moment I remembered it, I went back and read it and *instantly* knew what it meant! Never before could I figure out how Donne could be so triumphant over death, but now I knew! Before, the phrase "wee wake eternally" meant nothing to me.

Newly curious about John Donne, I did a little research and discovered that he was indeed a Christian and his poem talks about passing through death and spending eternity with God. When God is your destiny, death has no sting.

## WAKING UP

I continued watching Christian television and my hope continued to grow. The only time I had any kind of peace was when I heard people talk about God. About this same time an old girlfriend of mine started coming back around. She was pregnant and her boyfriend, the baby's father, had left her. With nowhere else to turn, she turned to me. I had a real struggle with this because I thought it was some kind of test. I was still bouncing back and forth as to whether I believed people were really people or demons. When she showed up, I had the first real human interaction I'd had with anyone other than the people I was with that first night. Being around someone else who was having trouble helped me see my own problems in a different light. I understood some of what she was going through and felt like I could help.

Up until now I had just been going through the motions of life and not really interacting with people. This odd circumstance put a human emotion into play that I hadn't experienced in months. I wasn't happy for someone else's struggle or anything like that, but it was her struggle that helped me look outside myself. Ultimately I walked with her through her decision and we parted ways. The benefit for me was that it brought me out of being so inwardly-focused on my own situation.

Helping my old girlfriend filled me with positive emotions of being useful. I felt compassion for her. I was not in love with her, but I could feel love for her as a human being. I began to ponder on what I was feeling. It was like I was waking up to real life again.

## NO LOVE IN HELL

This process paved the way for my next step out of hell. I began asking, "Can love exist in hell?" From what the devil and the demons had described about hell, I knew that love and compassion did not exist there. Using this reasoning I began to convince myself that quite possibly I *wasn't* dead. My feelings of love and compassion for my former girlfriend, as well as my conclusion that love could not exist in hell, filled me with a hope that helped me move closer to God. When everything else is gone, hope is the only thing that can keep you moving forward.

I had been utterly hopeless, convinced that I was doomed to hell. I had fully believed that I had been cut off from God with absolutely no chance of being saved. The devil doesn't have to get us to believe in hell or to renounce God; all he has to do is trick us into believing that there is no hope. Hope drives us and keeps us going. Without hope we are, well, hopeless.

*When everything else is gone, hope is the only thing that can keep you moving forward.*

Many people are convinced so strongly in their hopelessness that suicide seems the only viable option. It was no different with me. There were two times in the months of torture that I actually attempted suicide. The phrase, "A man's got to do what a man's got to do," kept ringing in my head. I took this to mean that I had to kill myself to pass to the lower depths of hell that I had doomed myself to. In one instance I swallowed several sleeping pills. Thankfully, I didn't take enough. Several times I thought of shooting myself and on one occasion in particular took a gun, pointed it toward my head and tried to squeeze the trigger. I can't explain what happened other than that I wasn't able to do it. I began to shake so uncontrollably that I dropped the gun.

Once hope finally came alive in me, I jumped on it with all my might. It was scary at first. I wasn't sure if I was just deceiving myself and that this was just another sick joke on me, but I was willing to endure the shame. The promise of what little hope I had was good enough for me. I was willing to be the butt of a demonic joke if it meant I could attain the prize I heard the TV preachers talking about. Pushing forward in my newfound state of thinking, I held on for dear life to that glimmer of light that had come alive in my heart.

## ANOTHER STEP TOWARD THE LIGHT

At some point I heard one of the television preachers talk about having a personal relationship with Jesus. I had no clue what that meant, yet somehow it felt right. I didn't know what to do, but I knew I wanted it. Although things in my life had improved, I still wrestled with thoughts and feelings of being dead. The growing hope inside me confused me; still, I was willing and determined to pursue what was in my heart. More and more, these new feelings seemed more real to me than the thoughts of being dead and in hell.

One of the preachers talked about praying, so I decided to try it. Since I didn't know what to say, I just opened my mouth and started talking. My prayer went something like this: "Jesus, I don't know if I am alive or dead and I don't know what to do, but I am asking You for help." As soon as I spoke those words, the light that I could see very faintly in my soul began to grow ever so slightly.

My next step out of hell was very exciting. It happened, appropriately enough, on Easter Sunday. Easter, of course, is the one Sunday in the year when even people who don't normally go to church go to church. That old girlfriend whom I had helped was going for Easter and invited me to come along. I immediately said yes. Strangely enough, I hadn't even thought about going to church up until now. Six months had passed since that fateful night, and I was experiencing longer and longer periods of time throughout the day when I wasn't thinking about being dead. My days would start out relatively well, but as soon as I heard, smelled or saw something that reminded me of hell (those triggers again), fear would creep in and I would have the battle in my head. It was a different battle now, however; it consisted of me telling myself that this new life of hope might be real and to keep going.

In church that Easter Sunday I had a strange but wonderful experience. I remember nothing of the sermon except for one very key statement the pastor made. Although I have replayed this event in my head over and over, to this day I don't know if the preacher actually said this or if God caused me to hear it. At some point in the sermon I saw the pastor's lips move as he said, "Even if you are in hell, God can save you."

*God can save you.*

That statement was like water being poured over my head. I literally felt all over me what I now know to be the presence of God. It was unlike anything I had ever felt before. I was so excited! I must have had a huge smile on my face or something because the preacher kept looking at me from then on. After the service he actually came over to speak with me and said that I looked like I was listening very intently.

I left the church that day with a greater sense of hope. Over and over I asked myself, "Is that true? Is it possible? Can God really save me from hell?" Up to this point I had been very confused about where I would go after this life. Now, for the first time, I began to see going to heaven as a real possibility. The preachers I saw on Christian television had been saying this for months, but this was the first time I actually believed it.

As I thought about what happened, I meditated on what had changed. I knew that I hadn't come back to life or done anything to deserve this; the only thing different was that I had started to see my situation differently. I didn't know how everything would play out, but I knew that I had to keep thinking that I was alive and focus on the fact that God could save me. The moment I made the decision to focus on God, I knew in my heart that He wanted to help me get out of this torment.

## ASCENT OUT OF HELL

Soon after that Easter service I went home and decided to talk to God more. It had felt so good the first time that I wanted to keep doing it. What happened next led to the decision that finally pulled me out of hell.

I was walking around the two sofas in my living room talking to God. They were positioned in an L-shape with walking room all the way around them. Essentially, I was doing laps around the living room. I said, "God, I want to believe You, but I don't know what to do. You're going to have to help me." Then I made the best decision in my life: I turned my every decision over to Him. I kept walking around the room, half the time experiencing excitement at the possibility and the other half fearful that maybe it wasn't real.

The more I talked to God, however, the more real it felt. I just kept telling Him that I couldn't do this and that if I was going to live, He was going to have to help me. I told Him that there was no way I could make it without His help. Then I asked for something that He had already promised me: that He would stay with me constantly and never leave me. Here I

was newly saved, still hearing demons, still facing mental torment, yet talking to God and knowing that He was there and
that He could hear me. The most exciting aspect of all in this
new experience was that, for the first time, *I could hear God.*

For months I had been communicating with the demonic forces on a spiritual level, so it wasn't much of a surprise
when I began to hear God speaking to
me. His manner of speaking was quite *For the first*
different from that of the demons. *time, I could*
Whenever I spoke to and heard the
demons, they always seemed to be
outside of me. When I spoke to and *hear God.*
heard God, however, I knew very dis-
tinctly that He was inside me. Once I turned my attention
into my own heart and heard God, it became very easy to
start shutting out the other voices.

Not only could I hear Him in my heart, I also could feel
Him with me. I took Him everywhere. Demons had been my
constant companions for six months, so having with me
another person I could not see was not so strange. There
was no question in my mind that Jesus was with me. I so
much enjoyed my new Friend that I would sit for hours on
my sofa and talk to Him. Before I ever went to church reg-
ularly or even read the Bible, I had an unshakable relationship with Jesus. Nothing could separate me from Him. At
times, the demons tried to communicate with me, but their
voices did not carry the same weight as before. Because
Jesus was with me, they couldn't get as close to me as previously. It was as if they were far away yelling at me but got
tired and gave up very quickly.

Day after day I would talk to Jesus. I would drive to work
and feel Him with me. I could be anywhere at all and know

He was right beside me. People sometimes ask me what we talked about, but I don't have any earth-shaking revelations to give them. Mostly I just thanked Him continually for saving my soul. I knew the magnitude of what He had done for me, and I could not stop thinking about Him.

For His part, Jesus simply communicated to me that He loved me and that He would never leave me. He didn't want anything from me and didn't ask me to do anything. He was perfectly content just being with me. He got great satisfaction from watching me daily walk more and more out of my mental torment. I spent the next six months just talking to Him and listening to Him tell me that He would always be with me.

## DRINKING FROM THE SOURCE

At some point I decided that I should probably try to read the Bible. I had my grandfather's old Bible, so one day I picked it up and began to read. I didn't know what to expect. I thought I was going to read about all these perfect people who knew God. Not knowing any better, I began reading the Bible from the front like any other book. When I got to the third chapter of Genesis, I was amazed. There, plain as day, was the evidence that the devil was nothing but a liar. I was so embarrassed that I had believed him for so long. How could I have been so stupid to believe what he had told me? I had spent six months walking around in a living hell on earth because of believing his lies—six months barely even questioning what I was told.

Anger at Satan rose up in my spirit, but Jesus immediately told me not to become angry. Lovingly He showed me how I had put myself in that position and that I should not become angry over something as insignificant as the devil.

I kept reading until I reached the place where Abraham gave his wife away in order to protect himself. This confused me. As I said, I had expected to read about perfect people who were following God and here's a guy pimping his wife! I put the Bible down and decided to just keep talking to Jesus to learn about God.

As strange as it may sound, I am thankful today that at that time I didn't go to church or form opinions about a book I didn't understand. My education about God came straight from the source. In my particular situation, He was the only one who could have really helped me. When I first started talking to God, I still believed that everyone around me was a demon. I wouldn't have listened to them anyway. I wasn't even sure about the preacher whose church I had attended on Easter or the TV preachers I had listened to for months. But I knew without question that the God inside me was real. That is where I first got to know Him.

Periodically I still tried to read the Bible. I would jump around in the Old Testament and just end up getting confused. One day while watching television, I heard a preacher talking about the New Testament and how the New Testament told about Jesus. Immediately I got my Bible out and looked for the New Testament. Sure enough, there it was. I began reading Matthew. In my mind's eye I can still see the room I was sitting in when I memorized my first scripture, Matthew 6:33: *"But seek ye first the kingdom of God, and his righteousness; and all these things shall be added unto you."*

God knew exactly what I needed to hear. I was worrying about how I was going to make it in life. For a year I had been wandering with no direction. Now I knew what I needed to do.

Since I was alive after all (and saved), I needed to plug back into society and try to make something of myself. In that time of need God eased my stress and took me right to the scripture I needed to hear.

## THE NON-RELIGIOUS JESUS

This was the first of a series of divine leadings to scriptures God wanted me to see. I was developing a relationship with this non-religious Jesus that I knew nothing about. At the beginning I had no idea that He was a real person who was concerned with my well-being. Until now I had turned away from God because all I knew of Christianity was a system of control with a bunch of rules. The last thing I expected was to encounter this non-religious Person.

*Jesus just wants to love us through everything.*

When I was in the living room marching around the sofas, I remember wondering what it really meant to be a Christian. I knew God could help me and that Jesus was with me, but I had no idea that a relationship with Jesus would be like this! I learned that Jesus is not concerned about *making* us do the right thing. He wants to be there for us and love us through everything. His power is not in the fact that He can destroy everything (even though He could) but in the fact that His love can change us.

Jesus doesn't want you to come to Him so He can make you into something you don't want to be; He just wants to love you through whatever situation you are in. Jesus simply wants to be there to encourage you. He knows that if you'll let His love into your heart it will change you. It's not that He gives you rules to follow that change you but the simple fact that He accepts you no matter what. He wants to be there for you and walk beside you through everything you may ever face.

The day I realized that Jesus would *never* condemn me is the day I knew that I was forever free from hell.

Again, God led me to a scripture:

*Because ye have said, We have made a covenant with death, and with hell are we at agreement; when the overflowing scourge shall pass through, it shall not come unto us: for we have made lies our refuge, and under falsehood have we hid ourselves: therefore thus saith the Lord GOD, Behold, I lay in Zion for a foundation a stone, a tried stone, a precious corner stone, a sure foundation: he that believeth shall not make haste....And your covenant with death shall be disannulled, and your agreement with hell shall not stand; when the overflowing scourge shall pass through, then ye shall be trodden down by it* (Isaiah 28:15-16, 18).

I was amazed. God showed me that He knew all about my deal with the devil. He knew that I had made a covenant to try to have a normal life. Now He was showing me that my deal with the devil was valid no more. In reality, there is no such thing as making a deal with the devil, but God knew where I was and showed me this to let me know that my future with death and hell had changed forever.

To solidify my freedom, God led me to a scripture in Colossians:

*Giving thanks unto the Father, which hath made us meet to be partakers of the inheritance of the saints in light: who hath delivered us from the power of darkness, and hath translated us into the kingdom of his dear Son: in whom we have redemption through his blood, even the forgiveness of sins* (Colossians 1:12-14).

When I saw this scripture, I could hardly contain myself. I felt that God had written it just for me. God knew that I was still struggling with fully believing that I was going to heaven, and He wanted me to be at peace. He wanted me to be totally free from the grip of Satan. God knew exactly where I was and provided the escape for me even before I was born.

Even though I understood what it meant to be delivered from the power of darkness, I didn't really understand the part about *"redemption through his blood."* So, as I was quickly learning to do, I asked God what it meant. He answered me immediately. What He showed me is forever engraved in my mind and in my heart. Blood redemption has to do with the most significant event in the history of mankind—*the cross.*

# Chapter Eight

# THE CROSS

—+— ≊◊≊ —+—

When I asked God to show me the meaning of the phrase *"redemption through his blood"* in Colossians 1:14, I wasn't prepared for what I was about to see.

I was sitting on my sofa in silence looking directly ahead. After asking God to reveal His Word to me, I shut my eyes and laid my head back. At first everything was dark. Then, off in the distance, I saw a faint light on top of what looked like a small mountain. The light was similar to the one I had first seen in the "black hole" of my heart. As I looked closer, I could tell that I was looking at a person. The scene moved closer and got larger as if through the zoom lens of a camera. The closer I got, the clearer the vision became. What I saw is etched in my mind forever. To this day I can shut my eyes and visualize that scene as if God had first shown it to me yesterday. Every time I look on that vision in my mind, it hits me with the same force it did the first time.

As the vision became crystal clear, I realized that I was looking at Jesus hanging on the cross. I stared in awe at how badly He was disfigured. The flesh of His body was ripped to shreds. There was not a single dry spot on Him because He was covered with His own blood. I was not repulsed as much as shocked. The gory scene had a strange attraction for me; I couldn't pull my eyes away but kept staring at every detail of His battered, tortured body. Jesus looked like He had been beaten for days and then hung on the cross like raw meat. His skin was almost completely gone. Huge spikes had been driven through His hands and feet to fasten Him to the cross, and I could see where the flesh around those hideous nails had torn from His weight. His hands were ripped almost completely to the top from hanging for so long.

*Never had I imagined that Jesus endured anything like this.*

I don't know how long I had been watching Him before I became aware of His tortured, labored breathing. If you have ever heard someone having a severe asthma attack, you have a good idea of how Jesus sounded. He could not take a full breath. Every breath was a painful, wheezing rasp from the fluid that was slowly filling His lungs. With every inhalation His body would lift slightly and then drop violently down as He exhaled. Already I was beginning to understand what God meant that my redemption was in Jesus' blood. I knew that Jesus had saved me, but it was only at this moment that I realized the incredible cost. Never had I imagined that Jesus endured anything like this.

As I continued to stare at Him in awed fascination, I finally noticed His eyes. When I first made eye contact, I realized that He had been looking at me the entire time. Even though I was, in a sense, looking back in time, I felt that Jesus could see me. While I considered this, God told me in my heart that Jesus indeed was looking at me. Two thousand years ago, while hanging on that cross, Jesus was thinking of me—and everyone else who would be saved through His death. The Bible doesn't say so, but I like to imagine Jesus thinking specifically about every single person who would ever live.

In that same moment I knew that even if I had been the only person to ever live, or the only person who ever need-ed my sins forgiven, Jesus still would have done this—*for me*. The same is true for you and for all of us. If you were the only person to be redeemed by what Jesus did on the cross, He still would have endured the pain. That's how great and how deep His love is. He loves you so much that if you were the only person to be saved through His death, He still would have chosen to die!

The more I watched, the more incredible it seemed that Jesus would do this for me. I felt so unworthy but, at the same time, so incredibly loved and valued. I squeezed my eyes tighter as blood continued to pour from His body. So much blood came out of Him that it formed a wave that rushed toward me and completely covered me. It not only covered me; it also infused into my body. It was as though Jesus' blood was seeping into my body and becoming my blood. I could literally feel His blood in my body.

## MADE NEW BY THE BLOOD

The Bible says that it is the blood of Jesus that washes away our sins and makes us clean and righteous. This means we no longer have to try to be righteous on our own. If we accept fully what Jesus did on the cross for us, we are completely perfect. When God looks at us, He sees the blood of Jesus. The shedding of blood was a must in the Old Testament for atonement, but Jesus' sacrifice was much more precious. His sacrifice was once and for all. There is no going back on what He did. Jesus' death on the cross can never be repeated. Nor does it need to be.

After this stunning vision, I now knew what Jesus had done for me. I was a new person freed from hell forever. I was a new creature, just as the Bible says:

*Therefore if any man be in Christ, he is a new creature: old things are passed away; behold, all things are become new* (2 Corinthians 5:17).

I was sinful and Jesus made me perfect. Jesus was perfect and became sin for me.

*For he hath made him to be sin for us, who knew no sin; that we might be made the righteousness of God in him* (2 Corinthians 5:21).

## A PERSONAL SAVIOR

The vision finally faded away, but its image will be with me forever. I was still amazed that Jesus had done this for me. I thought about a situation with a friend of mine who had been hurt by the actions of another person and had taken it incredibly personally. All he could say was, "*He* did that to me...*he* did that to me. I wouldn't care if it was someone else, but *he* did that to me!" Except for the hurt, I could say the same thing about Jesus. I just kept telling myself,

"Jesus did that for *me*! Jesus did that for *me*!" I personalized what Jesus had done for me on the cross.

Little did I know the great favor I was doing for myself by writing this truth on my heart and making it personal. That was the moment that allowed me to believe for the rest of my life that Jesus died for me. He did it not just because it was His Father's will and not just because He wanted to save the world. More personally, Jesus died on the cross because He wanted to save *me*, and He still would have done it if it was *only* for me.

*Jesus died on the cross because He wanted to save me.*

He would have done it for you too. I don't know where you stand with Jesus, but let me ask you this question: "Is Jesus your *personal* Savior?" You may know Him as your Lord, but have you ever really *personalized* what He did for you? If you haven't, let me suggest that you lay this book down and begin now to visualize Jesus dying for you—*just* for you. Ask the Lord to help you with this. Make it as personal as possible. See Jesus thinking about you—personally. See Him carrying your sin—personally. See Jesus enduring the punishment for *your* sin—personally. See Him hanging in agony because of His love for you—personally.

I promise you, if you are struggling with any aspect of your walk with God, this will empower you to live a godly life more than anything else you could ever do. Believing on a personal level what Jesus did for you is the very heart of the Gospel.

Jesus not only paid the price for your salvation on the cross, Isaiah also told us that He took all of our sicknesses and diseases so we can enjoy good health:

*Surely he hath borne our griefs, and carried our sorrows: yet we did esteem him stricken, smitten of God, and afflicted. But he was wounded for our transgressions, he was bruised for our iniquities: the chastisement of our peace was upon him; and with his stripes we are healed* (Isaiah 53:4-5).

Jesus gave up His perfect nature and became sin for us, but He also gave up His perfect health and became our sicknesses. While on the cross, Jesus literally bore the effects of all sickness and disease. This is one reason He was so grotesquely disfigured while hanging on the cross. Isaiah 52:14 says *"his visage was so marred more than any man, and his form more than the sons of men."*

It wasn't just Jesus' body up there on the cross with its own effects; He also was carrying the sin of the world. God literally poured out His wrath and judgment of all sin on Jesus so we wouldn't have to face it. Jesus was the only human qualified to pay this price because He was perfect.

God desires to have us in His family, but to dwell in God's presence we have to be perfect. I'm not perfect and neither are you. Without Jesus we all stand guilty before God: *"For all have sinned, and come short of the glory of God"* (Romans 3:23). When we place our faith in Jesus as our personal Savior, His blood takes away our sin and sets us free: *"There is therefore now no condemnation to them which are in Christ Jesus, who walk not after the flesh, but after the Spirit. For the law of the Spirit of life in Christ Jesus hath made me free from the law of sin and death"* (Romans 8:1-2).

Jesus so looked forward to having us as brothers and sisters that He was willing to endure the cross. Hebrews 12:2

tells us that Jesus *"for the joy that was set before him endured the cross, despising the shame, and is set down at the right hand of the throne of God."*

In Christ, we now have the full righteousness of God: *"But now the righteousness of God without the law is manifested, being witnessed by the law and the prophets; even the righteousness of God which is by faith of Jesus Christ unto all and upon all them that believe"* (Romans 3:21-22).

Accepting Jesus Christ as our Savior gives us new life. The Bible calls it being "born again" or "born from above." Receiving new life makes us new creations in Christ: *"Therefore if any man be in Christ, he is a new creature: old things are passed away; behold, all things are become new"* (2 Corinthians 5:17).

We have taken on Jesus and are now new creatures and perfect in God's eyes. When God looks at a believer, He sees someone as holy and spotless as Jesus. The Bible says that as Jesus is now, so are we in Him. Don't let your Christian faith be only about going to heaven and nothing more. Search the New Testament, especially the epistles, to find out what God's Word says about our new identity in Christ. Make the cross of Christ real and personal in your life and ask the Lord to empower you to live the kind of life that He has promised you.

## HELL IS NOT GOD'S CHOICE

"If God loves us so much, why does He send people to hell?" I couldn't begin to count the number of times I've heard this question. On the surface it sounds logical: How could a loving God ever send anyone to as horrible a place as hell? In light of the cross of Christ, there is no doubt that God loves us, so the answer to the hell question must have nothing to do with God's love.

Here's the answer: *God does not send anyone to hell.* All those who are in hell are there by their own choice as the consequence of their own decision to reject God. The Bible says that hell was created as a place of confinement and judgment for the devil and his angels (see Matthew 25:41).

*God does not send anyone to hell.*

It was never God's intention or choice for any human being to go to hell.

Going to hell has nothing to do with God sending people there. Before I accepted Jesus I knew I was on my way to hell, and it had nothing to do with God making a decision. My destiny before Jesus had everything to do with *my* decisions. God is not some judgmental figure sitting on a throne deciding who will spend eternity with Him and who will spend eternity cut off from Him. God gave each of us a will of our own with which we choose our own destiny. Unfortunately, because of human pride, many people will end up in an eternity cut off from God.

Today it seems inconceivable to me how anyone could reject God, the Father of love and Creator of all that is good, for the brief satisfaction of fulfilling his or her own selfish desires. Yet, that is what happens every second of every day. It's a testimony to the strength of human will and the depth of human pride. Sometimes, unfortunately, people are turned away from God because of what they see in other people, particularly people who claim to know Jesus.

Jesus commissioned His followers to take His message to the entire world. He asked His immediate disciples to go and make other disciples. Jesus wanted His followers to go and show the same kind of compassion and love that He showed while He was walking the earth.

In the 2,000 years since, the church has attempted hundreds, if not millions, of tactics to reach people with only moderate success. Today, of the six billion people on earth, less than one-third are Christians. Why is that? How could so many people reject such infinite, perfect love? How could so many people willingly pass into eternity without God? I would like to think that Jesus meets people at the point of death to give them one last chance, but the Bible provides no evidence or support for such an idea. In fact, the Bible says that this life is our only opportunity to come to Christ: *"And as it is appointed unto men once to die, but after this the judgment: so Christ was once offered to bear the sins of many; and unto them that look for him shall he appear the second time without sin unto salvation"* (Hebrews 9:27-28).

Given these statistics, this means that the majority of the world's population is passing into eternity without Jesus. Think of it—most of the people in the world are going to hell! This is alarming! This is tragic! God created a world in perfect harmony and peace so that He could have a family. He knew that it was not truly a family without free will, so He gave us that freedom when He created us. Sadly, on the basis of that freedom, God is losing a large portion of His family. Precious human souls are entering hell every second. They are experiencing the same torment, except that theirs is all too real and all too eternal. They won't "snap out of it" and get another chance. They will forever be in emotional and physical torment because they didn't accept the love that Jesus expressed to them on the cross.

This doesn't have to be the destiny of the rest of mankind. As Christians we can change the eternal destiny of human souls. We have the power within us through the Holy Spirit to show people the love of God. We can intercept them while they are on their way to a destiny that no one desires. But what are we doing to change it? None of us can change the world by ourselves, but we can make an impact in the lives of people around us. What are we doing to help our loved ones and friends and neighbors and work colleagues know the love of God and come to Jesus for forgiveness of their sins?

Jesus risked everything to gain us as family members. While His body was in the grave, He descended into hell so we wouldn't have to. Are you willing to sacrifice a little comfort in order to change the path of someone close to you? The Bible says that it's the goodness of God that brings people to repentance. You don't have to be a scholar or a physicist who can intellectually prove the existence of God. All you have to do is be able to tell people how good God is—how good He has been to you.

Tell them that God is not an angry God ready to strike them down with a lightning bolt, but a loving Father who desires a love relationship with them. Tell them that God's wrath against sin is forever satisfied through Jesus' sacrifice on the cross. Now that Jesus has paid the penalty for every soul that has ever lived or ever will live, God's wrath is satisfied. Jesus is the "*propitiation*," or atoning sacrifice, for our sins (see Romans 3:25; 1 John 2:2; 4:10). Jesus' death on the cross satisfied God's holy demand for judgment of sin.

This means that Jesus has already dealt with the righteousness issue. Whenever we talk to people about Jesus, we should focus not on what they need to do but on what He has already done. I firmly believe that many of the people who have passed into eternity without God would have chosen God had they heard the truth about His love and how it was demonstrated so dramatically and so completely at the cross.

I cannot stress enough that God is not some mean old tyrant who zaps people into hell for not obeying Him. The truth is that if our soul is not regenerated in righteousness through Jesus, we cannot coexist with a righteous and holy God. It's *What will* as simple as light and dark. Darkness can- *you do?* not coexist with light. If a human soul has not received the light of Jesus, it cannot be in the presence of God who is true light. The only way we can live in and enjoy God's presence is for our sin to be removed and replaced with righteousness, and the only way that can happen is through faith in Christ for the cleansing of our sins by His blood.

Again I ask, what will you do to ensure that the people around you will not pass into eternity without knowing the truth about what Jesus did for them on the cross? We have the power of the Holy Spirit working in us, but it's up to us to act on that power and let Him work through us. We can either let the power of God work through us or we can squelch it. The choice is ours, and we decide every day in one way or another.

I realize that is a bold statement, but think about it for a minute. If God didn't work through us, then why wouldn't He just come down and save everyone? The answer comes back to free will. The Bible says that God has been revealed to everyone. No one has an excuse. No one will go into eternity saying that he or she didn't hear about God because nature itself points to the existence of God. This doesn't mean that we shouldn't be an influence in addition to what God has revealed; it just means that everyone knows about God. No matter how vehemently someone insists that he doesn't believe in God, the Bible states that God has been revealed to every man.

This encourages me because it means I have something to work with. I don't have to persuade someone of God's love. All I have to do is help people connect to what has already been revealed to them. The truth is already in everyone; we just get to take part in helping people uncover the truth that is already there. I'm not saying that everyone is already saved or will be saved. I'm just saying that, deep down, every man, woman and child already knows that God is real. This is God's way of giving us the decision and why we are accountable to Him for it.

God is not in heaven busily deciding who will be His children and who won't. He has already revealed Himself to everyone and it is up to us who know Him to help people connect with that knowledge no matter how deeply they may have suppressed it. What will you do to help people discover the truth already in them? What will you do to ensure that your friends, family and neighbors will not spend eternity without God? What will you do to make sure they know about the awesome work of love that Jesus performed for them on the cross? What will you do to help break the cycle of death that has dominated human history since the fall of man in the Garden of Eden?

# Chapter Nine

# DEATH OBSESSION

Jesus is sometimes called the Great Physician. In my case He was the Great Psychologist. He was able to bring me successfully through what some would describe as a psychotic state. About a year after my experience, when I began to function normally again, I started researching what had happened to me. In the process I learned some very interesting things about my own situation as well as mankind's uneasy relationship with questions of life and death.

Most people prefer to view life in terms of black or white, right or wrong, cut and dried with no "gray" areas of uncertainty, even if their own experience suggests otherwise. We Americans tend to be "either-or" thinkers, meaning that matters are either totally one way or totally the other. After researching similar cases to mine and talking to professionals, I discovered that had I sought professional help, I would have been diagnosed as schizophrenic. My particular bout with schizophrenia would have been classified as a chemical imbalance due to over-toxification—basically, a drug overdose.

While physiologically there is certainly truth to that, most professionals would have left it at that with no regard to the possibility of any involvement from the supernatural realm. The psychological and psychiatric disciplines by and large rule out any chance of supernatural intervention as a possibility. These professions study the mind and that's it. Every mental or emotional aberration is biochemically based and influenced by environment and/or past life experiences. Little or no allowance is given to the spiritual realm as a contributing factor. Indeed, for many professionals in these fields, any reference by a patient to the spiritual realm throws up a red flag. If someone starts talking about the devil to one of these professionals, medication usually follows.

Despite what many of these secular psychological and psychiatric professionals would say, my encounters with Satan and demons were *real*. They actually took place. The LSD I took put my mind in an altered state of consciousness that made me especially susceptible and vulnerable to contact by and influence from the supernatural world. Furthermore, without Christ in my heart, I had no spiritual defense against those demonic encounters and no framework for discerning and rejecting the lies I was told.

Something else I discovered in my research is that I was not the first person to experience this kind of thing—and I won't be the last. In fact, I found that experiences such as mine have been researched, studied and written about for centuries. I was obsessed with death to the point of believing that I *was* dead and in hell and condemned to die repeatedly in an endless cycle. My research uncovered many extraordinary stories of near-death experiences as well as ancient practices and multiple religions that have death at their center.

Death is a frightening yet engaging and ultimately irresistible topic for man because it touches every one of us. The one thing that we all share in common as human beings is that we're going to die. Christianity, on the authority of the Word of God, promises that all who trust in Christ will never taste death—the only faith system in the world that offers such assurance. When we place our faith in Christ, we pass from death to life—spiritual life that has no end. Jesus said:

> *Verily, verily, I say unto you, He that heareth my word, and believeth on him that sent me, hath everlasting life, and shall not come into condemnation; but is passed from death unto life* (John 5:24).

Did you catch that? We who believe in Christ will *not* be condemned and have *already* passed from death to life! Eternal life is a *present reality* for us! Such a truth removes all fear of death because death becomes simply a gateway to a higher level of life and to the immediate and direct presence of God. The apostle Paul wrote:

> *We are confident, I say, and willing rather to be absent from the body, and to be present with the Lord* (2 Corinthians 5:8).

## THERE'S GOT TO BE SOMETHING MORE

By far the most interesting—and sometimes chilling—areas I uncovered in my research were religions and belief systems that seemed to be centered on the death experience. Every religion broaches the topic of death at some point. Many ancient books have been written about the subject. The *Tibetan Book of the Dead* and the *Egyptian Book of the Dead* are probably the two most well-known, while the *Ars Moriendi* is another key book in the field. All these writings make many similar points. They stress purity, self-development, enriching life, becoming a better person and attaining enlightenment, but stripped down to their essentials they all focus on one thing: being prepared for death.

Death-related experiences, communicating with spirits and supernatural phenomena can be traced to the very beginning of man's history and even earlier. Even the archaeological remains of prehistoric cultures reveal evidence of cultic rituals regarding the dead. Egyptian pharaohs were buried with massive amounts of wealth so they could be comfortable in the afterlife. Shamans would purposefully become sick and seclude themselves for days to reach the point of death in hopes of communicating with the other side.

When LSD first came on the scene, it was used by the psychology and psychiatry fields to explore the human psyche. Many of these tests resulted in accounts of the participant having a deep religious experience. Reports of demonic attack, inhuman torture and hellish visions were common. Some even claimed to have communicated with angels and even God.

Throughout time humans have sought to understand what lies beyond death. Thrill seekers and adrenaline junkies have developed new kinds of religions that don't look like a typical religion but are designed to draw closer to the meaning of life. All these belief systems, studies, stunts and desires reveal that man is deeply interested— even obsessed—with death and the afterlife. Perhaps no question has engaged the mind of man more consistently and thorough- ly than the question of what awaits us after this physical life.

*We have an innate drive to understand the afterlife.*

Man possesses an innate drive to understand the afterlife. This drive arises in part because of our natural, God-given curiosity to understand life and the world around us. Our obsession with life and death issues derives also from the fact that we were created orig- inally to be eternal beings but that condition was lost at the fall of man in the Garden of Eden. Even though our brains don't always acknowledge it, our hearts know that there is more to life and existence than just this physical realm. We were made for eternity and our hearts yearn to return there.

## WHICH COMES FIRST, DEATH OR LIFE?

With the exception of Christianity, all the religions and belief systems of the world focus on preparing for death. Although most of the adherents of those religions would not characterize them that way, it is true just the same. On the surface, Buddhism, Hinduism and other Eastern religions seem very noble in the sense that they appear to be about pure and holy living. The degree to which they emphasize the meaninglessness of worldly pursuits is very attractive to someone questioning the value of life and how it relates to our carnal world. There is much focus and attention given to physical health and cleansing.

Deep meditation is also a staple of many of the world's religions. Meditation usually focuses on purity, light, wellness and transcending the ego. Ego loss is a paramount goal of many of these religions. Beneath all these seemingly enlightened rituals and practices lies a darker undercurrent of pessimism and hopelessness because of the inescapability of death. Ultimately, the goal of purity, clean living, meditation and all the other rituals of these religions is to cross favorably into the afterlife. Buddhists, Hindus and others live the way they do in hopes of dying the way they desire. Life, then, becomes nothing more than extended preparation for death.

*Christianity's view on life and death set it apart from all other religions.*

They believe that living right, treating people right and connecting to the "higher being" or intelligence in the universe will cause their death experience to be good. Granted, living right and peacefully can carve out an enjoyable life and has its benefits on this earth, but ultimately the importance of these actions lies more in their effect on one's afterlife. Reincarnation, a virtually endless cycle of death and rebirth, awaits the soul that does not perform righteously while alive. A righteous soul will at death break the karmic cycle and attain a higher level of existence and consciousness, commonly known as *nirvana*.

Sadly enough, although they use different terminologies, many Christians have a similar view that their "performance" in life is what causes God to accept them. This is a false view. Properly understood, the way Christianity views life and death is what sets it apart from all other religions and belief systems in the world.

Rather than focusing on preparing for death, as do all the other belief systems of the world, Christianity focuses on preparing for *life.* Instead of beginning with life and moving toward death, the Christian faith *begins* with death and moves toward *life.* The heart of the Christian faith is the *death* of Jesus Christ for the sins of all mankind. At the same time, the starting point for all of us who choose to follow Christ is *also* a *death:* our death to sin, self-will and our old way of life in disobedience to God. It is only when we acknowledge the fact of our spiritual death that we can find our true life in Jesus Christ. Paul expressed this truth this way in Galatians:

*I am crucified with Christ: nevertheless I live; yet not I, but Christ liveth in me: and the life which I now live in the flesh I live by the faith of the Son of God, who loved me, and gave himself for me* (Galatians 2:20).

And to the Romans he wrote:

*Know ye not, that so many of us as were baptized into Jesus Christ were baptized into his death? Therefore we are buried with him by baptism into death: that like as Christ was raised up from the dead by the glory of the Father, even so we also should walk in newness of life....Likewise reckon ye also yourselves to be dead indeed unto sin, but alive unto God through Jesus Christ our Lord* (Romans 6:3-4, 11).

Other religions teach that you must live well in order to die well. Christianity teaches that you must die well in order to live well. All religious belief systems, including Christianity, emphasize the importance of living right and doing good works. The difference lies in the fact that in other religions people live right in the *hope* of finding life while Christians live right because they already *have* life.

Certainly, we should live right and treat others lovingly, but that is not what gets us into heaven. The blood of Jesus *alone* is what will get us there and guarantees us the "good death" that we all desire. Other religions stress performance and good works as the keys to eternal life. Christianity is not about "performance" but about what Jesus did for us on the cross. In other religions, how you live determines how you die. In Christianity, how you die determines how (and whether) you live.

## RELIGION OR RELATIONSHIP?

Let's make a comparison for better understanding. Tai Chi is a meditative exercise of the Chinese religion Taoism and is excellent for promoting physical and mental health and energy. Taoists believe in a creative intelligence that they describe as "The Way." They define "The Way" in terms very similar to the Greek term *logos*, which is usually translated as "the word." The actual meaning of *logos* goes much deeper, referring not to just words themselves but also to the logic, ideas and concepts that lie behind the words.

For example, the *logos* of God would be the logic that God put into motion when He created the world. Science and other studies into the way our world works are only seeing the natural, logical systems that God created to cause our world to function. The Bible says that God can be known by watching nature. The *logos* undergirds God's creation and keeps its natural functions in harmony. Taoism believes in this level of *logos* ("The Way") but fails to understand the next level, which the Bible reveals.

The Gospel of John opens with these words: *"In the beginning was the Word [logos], and the Word [logos] was with God, and the Word [logos] was God"* (John 1:1). A little later it says, *"And the Word [logos] was made flesh, and dwelt among us, (and we beheld his glory, the glory as of the only begotten of the Father,) full of grace and truth"* (John 1:14). The "Word" or *logos* that became was Jesus. He was and is the "logic" that sustains everything that is. Try wrapping your mind around that! Jesus is much more than what we traditionally think He is.

I said all of that to say this: Taoism, along with several other religions, accepts the idea that a creative intelligence designed our existence but will not accept the idea of that creative intelligence becoming a man and ultimately dying for our sins to regenerate our fallen souls. The result of this rejection of the Word made flesh is a religion of works and performance designed with the hope of someday being able to coexist with that creative intelligence in the afterlife. Do you see the lack of confidence and *true* hope for the future that come from rejecting the reality and sin-cleansing death of Jesus Christ?

Here is how Tai Chi works (supposedly): Tai Chi is a series of movements that stimulates energy in the body. The Chinese call this energy, "chi." One of the purposes of Tai Chi is to cultivate and accumulate "chi" in the body. Chi cultivation has many functions, among which are quicker healing for the body and the promotion of general good health and balance. There is a deeper purpose for chi, however. Your local Tai Chi instructor may not tell you this, but the ultimate purpose for accumulating chi is to take the participant across the great expanse of death into the realm of nirvana. Nirvana is the Eastern religion counterpart to heaven and is a state of non-conscious existence where one is freed from the karmic cycle and absorbed into the one great creative intelligence. Individual consciousness and personality are lost when nirvana is obtained.

How could the spiritual nature of man degrade to the point where people are willing to believe that they can live a good enough life on earth to accumulate enough energy to pass safely through death to the life beyond in their own strength? Most people by and large will accept the idea of God but won't accept His revelation of the way of salvation through His Son, Jesus Christ. Why not? The spiritual nature of man has been corrupted by sin and his ability to understand spiritual truth on his own has been destroyed. This makes him vulnerable and susceptible to lies and deception by Satan and his demonic forces, just as I was.

The purpose of life is not to follow a religion that seeks to reach God and the afterlife by our own efforts. The purpose of life is to enter into a personal relationship with our Creator that will last forever. God loves us and initiates and pursues just such a relationship with us. He was serious enough about this relationship to sacrifice His Son on the cross so that the sin separating us from Him could be removed and we could enter into fellowship with Him. God did everything necessary to make it easy for us to have a relationship with Him. Unfortunately, our lack of self-worth and simple lack of understanding continually drive us to perform in an effort to self-validate our salvation.

If you have been pursuing eternal bliss apart from Jesus, consider this: All religions require right living on the part of their adherents. In order to die favorably, each person must attain an impossible level of righteousness. Christ offers a different way. God knew that sinful mankind could not be "good" enough to pass into eternity and reach heaven on his own. So He sent His Son, Jesus—His wisdom—to live perfectly among us so that His sinless life would be an acceptable

*Sin is a blood disease.*

sacrifice to pay the penalty for our sins. Jesus faced the pressure and temptations of this life and lived *perfectly*.

Most religions acknowledge that Jesus was a good man, a wise teacher and an excellent moral example to live up to, but they miss the main point. The crux of Jesus' incarnation was to qualify us for heaven *apart from* the quality of our soul. Our eternity does *not* depend on what we do in this life. It is impossible for us to cleanse ourselves of sin so that we can coexist with a sinless and holy God. No amount of performance will do because performance does nothing about the sin problem.

Sin is a blood disease that cannot be cured by good works or performance any more than cancer can be cured by taking up jogging. The only way to "cure" the blood disease of sin is to receive a complete transfusion of healthy, sinless blood, and the only source of such blood is the blood of Jesus. Without the blood of Jesus, no one can pass through death unscathed.

If you choose to allow Jesus to come into your heart and make you righteous by His blood, you will find that this life is much more enjoyable and stress-free. Actually, what will happen is that His strength will begin to empower you and you will have His help to live righteously. Other religions rely on the strength of the individual, but a relationship with Jesus relies on His strength. Do you want to spend the rest of your life trying to make it in your own strength and ability or in the strength and ability of the only perfect man who has ever lived? Do you want your eternal destiny to be determined by your performance or by the blood of Jesus, which is sufficient to wash away your sin and make you righteous in God's eyes? The choice is yours. Which way will you choose?

No matter what you are facing, Jesus can bring you out. I was in the most extreme situation where I thought there was no hope, but Jesus lovingly brought me to the point where I could safely accept His reality. At the time I encountered Jesus, my psyche was extremely fragile. Gently and tenderly, Jesus led me through the process of walking in truth. He can do the same for you.

So often we create our own hell on earth by continually rejecting the love and grace of God and getting ourselves stuck in the same cycle of repeated sin. For a while we keep fooling ourselves with the belief that we can get out on our own, but eventually we develop a mind-set in which we accept where we are and resign ourselves to the "reality" that we will never get out. Psychologically, we rule out the possibility that Jesus can help us in that particular area. That is why it is important for us to submit to the Great Psychologist and let Him develop in us a new way of thinking. God is bigger than our thinking. Jesus is smarter than we are. He knows just how to help us walk out of anything. The key is in believing that Jesus is able to do so and that

He wants to. He doesn't expect us to conquer sin in our strength but to believe that He has already conquered it on our behalf.

Why do we find this so hard to do, even after we become Christians? Part of the reason lies in the fact that our hearts and minds have been corrupted through the influence and temptation of Satan, who is a liar and the father of lies, and whose secret sin goes back to the beginning of time.

# Chapter Ten

# SATAN'S SECRET SIN

⊶ ⚏◈⚏ ⊷

So what's the deal with the devil anyway? Why does he do what he does? Why does he want to mess with people and make their lives miserable? If he hates man so much, then why doesn't he just kill us all? The answer is simple: *He can't.* Satan lacks both the authority and the power to kill any of us on his own initiative. In fact, the only power Satan has over us is the power we give him. Even then, his only power is in our willingness to believe his lies. Many people talk about being "possessed" by the devil or by a demon. There is no such thing as possession; only *influence.*

That influence can be formidable. For instance, Satan is a thief who tries to "steal" the Word of God from a person's heart so that it cannot take root and lead to life transformation. Jesus said, *"The thief cometh not, but for to steal, and to kill, and to destroy"* (John 10:10a). In the parable of the sower and

127

the seed, Jesus talks about the "seed" of the Word being sown on "hard ground," only to have the birds (representing Satan, the evil one) eat the seed before it can take root (see Matthew 13:3-23). Satan tries to steal the Word by sowing lies in our minds and seeking to distract us by clouding our minds with worldly philosophy and tempting us with worldly things.

When Satan does these things, he is simply acting according to his nature and his original intent. In the very beginning, however, it was not this way. Although the Bible is not explicit about Satan's origin and original nature, we infer from several scriptures that he was originally created by God as an archangel and was one of the most beautiful and splendid beings in the spiritual realm. At that time, he was not known as Satan, which means "adversary" and describes his nature after his fall. Isaiah 14:12 refers to him as "Lucifer," a Latin word borrowed from the Latin translation of the Bible known as the Vulgate and that means "morning star."

How did Lucifer fall from his high position in the angelic hierarchy? A few verses from the book of Ezekiel are sufficient to describe what happened:

> Son of man, say unto the prince of Tyrus, Thus saith the Lord GOD; Because thine heart is lifted up, and thou hast said, I am a God, I sit in the seat of God, in the midst of the seas; yet thou art a man, and not God, though thou set thine heart as the heart of God:...Thou art the anointed cherub that covereth; and I have set thee so: thou wast upon the holy mountain of God; thou hast walked up and down in the midst of the stones of fire. Thou wast perfect in thy ways from the day that thou wast created, till iniquity was found in

*thee....Thine heart was lifted up because of thy beau-
ty, thou hast corrupted thy wisdom by reason of thy
brightness: I will cast thee to the ground, I will lay thee
before kings, that they may behold thee* (Ezekiel 28:2,
14-15, 17).

Lucifer was overcome by pride and thought he could exalt
himself above God. He wanted to sit in the throne of God; he
wanted God's power. If this sounds familiar, it is because he
tempted Eve the same way in the Garden of Eden by promis-
ing her that if she ate the fruit from the forbidden tree, she
would be like God. Satan used his own false beliefs, the very
beliefs that had led to his own downfall, to entice Eve.

But wait a minute; this doesn't make much sense! How
could God create an angel that had a pride issue? How
could God create such a powerful being that would turn his
back on Him?

The secret lies in Satan's first encounter with man. The
Bible describes a war in heaven where Lucifer and a third of
the angels rebelled against God and were cast out of heaven.
It's easy to conclude that Satan looked at himself, got a
swelled head and jumped to the conclusion that he could overthrow God. But is that what *really* happened? What happened
before the war in heaven? What would cause Satan to go that
far? How could he have gone from one of the most powerful
angels to fighting against God? What was Satan's "secret sin"?

## "GOD'S HOLDING OUT ON YOU"

Sin begins on the inside. I'm sure we all agree that God
did not create Satan with an evil nature. So what happened?

We can find some clues in Genesis chapter 3 in the account of Satan's first contact with humans.

*Now the serpent was more subtle than any beast of the field which the LORD God had made. And he said unto the woman, Yea, hath God said, Ye shall not eat of every tree of the garden?* (Genesis 3:1).

Notice how Satan questions God's integrity and authority right off the bat. But what is the nature of this questioning? What led him to propose this kind of temptation? Look at verse 5:

*For God doth know that in the day ye eat thereof, then your eyes shall be opened, and ye shall be as gods, knowing good and evil* (Genesis 3:5).

Let me paraphrase what Satan was saying to Eve.

"God knows the real truth. He's holding out on you. He really hasn't given you this garden and paradise with no strings attached. God knows there is more. Why else would He put this tree here? Think about it; if God has given you everything, then why put this tree here and then tell you not to eat its fruit? There's something more, something you don't have, something that God doesn't want you to know. You can be as powerful as God and rule yourself. You don't need Him. You can be your own God."

Satan tricked Eve into believing the same thing that had brought about his own fall. Satan fell because he thought God was not giving him what he deserved. Look again at

Ezekiel 28:15: *"Thou wast perfect in thy ways from the day that thou wast created,* **till iniquity was found in thee.***"*

The word *iniquity* in the original Hebrew contains a few revealing truths about what was going on in Satan's thinking. Traditionally, the word *iniquity* is translated as wickedness, but here it has to do with deprivation. Satan felt deprived of something. He was standing in the face of God in all His glory and felt a sense of lack. Can you imagine that? Here's Lucifer, standing in front of Jehovah *Sin begins on the inside.* Jireh, the Provider, and he convinces himself that something is missing. He deludes himself with this thought to the degree that he is willing to fight over it. He is willing to throw everything away just to prove himself right.

## UNBELIEF: SATAN'S SECRET SIN

The Bible isn't clear about what happened in the heavens before the creation of man, but we can deduce some things from a few other scriptures. Hebrews 1:14 says that angels are ministering spirits to the *"heirs of salvation."* We see angels ministering to Jesus in His earthly life. The spiritual realm was created before man was created. I can see the sequence of events unfolding something like this (please understand, this is only my speculation): God created the spiritual realm containing various degrees of angels, including archangels, of which Lucifer was one. Lucifer probably started getting prideful about his beauty and his standing in the kingdom of God before he even knew about man. At some point, God revealed His plan for creating man. Man was to be God's family. Man would be closer to God even than the angels. In fact, God told the angels that their job would be to *serve* man.

Can you imagine how such an idea must have infuriated Lucifer? This could have been one contributing factor in Lucifer's decision to drive a wedge, so to speak, between God and man. (Remember, I'm only speculating.)

Whatever happened and whatever the reason, Lucifer was still so convinced of his own lies and judgments about God that he pushed them on to Adam and

*Lucifer passed his own lie on to Adam and Eve.*

Eve. But was that his secret sin? Was his desire to kill man and destroy God's family the original motivation for his sin? Certainly it was a result of his sin, but let's take this issue down to its basic root.

Truth is always discovered when we go down to the most basic root of an issue. The thing that caused Lucifer to fall is actually the very same thing that causes us to fall. It's the reason people are going to hell minute by minute. It's the reason some people can't get healed. It's the reason some people stay in the same sin all their lives. It's the reason we have denominations that fight against each other. It's the reason we don't live the abundant life. Satan's secret sin is the very same issue that you and I struggle with all the time.

Reduced to its most rudimentary level, Satan's secret sin is simply one thing: *unbelief.*

But isn't that *too* simple? That's exactly my point. It all starts right there. Lucifer didn't believe God. God created His kingdom and appointed the angels to their positions. After creating Lucifer and assigning him his position, Lucifer began to question God. Questioning God is not necessarily a bad thing if you are truly searching for the truth and want to make sure you have understood Him correctly, but to conclude that God is wrong or has lied is to commit a grave and drastic error. Satan's words to Eve and the tactic he used suggest that he believed God was lying. In short, Satan didn't believe God, and he passed his sin to mankind when he tricked Eve into disobeying God.

## UNBELIEF SEPARATES US FROM THE ABUNDANT LIFE

Unbelief is the cancer that destroyed the paradise God created for us. Unbelief is the seed within our own hearts that leads us away from what God has promised. You might be saying, "But I believe God; this doesn't make any sense." By and large that may be true, but if all of God's promises are yes and amen, then why are you not walking in the fullness of what you know is yours? If you are, congratulations, but you're an exception in Christianity today.

Sure we believe in God. Yes, we believe God exists. Absolutely, we believe Jesus is our salvation because of what He did on the cross. But what about everyday life? I'm not saying that we should never have any trouble. On the contrary, Jesus promised that we *would* have trouble. I'm just saying that in many areas of our lives we do not walk in fullness because we are not fully convinced that God has redeemed those areas. Consequently, we have never fully connected to the abundant life that God has provided us through the blood of Jesus.

Look at the area of health, for example. God has given us divine life and healing in Jesus. Jesus took all of our pain, sickness and sorrow on the cross. Isaiah 53:5 says,

*"But he was wounded for our transgressions, he was bruised for our iniquities: the chastisement of our peace was upon him; and with his stripes we are healed."*

This means that we are qualified to be healed because of what Jesus endured for us on the cross. First John 4:17 says, *"Herein is our love made perfect, that we may have boldness in the day of judgment: because as he is, so are we in this world."* We're not like Jesus was when He was walking the earth; we are like the way He is now. He has given us His life. God reckoned us dead with Jesus on the cross. We were buried with Him and raised with Him by the power of His resurrection. The Bible tells us that we are complete now in Christ.

*And ye are complete in him, which is the head of all principality and power: in whom also ye are circumcised with the circumcision made without hands, in putting off the body of the sins of the flesh by the circumcision of Christ: buried with him in baptism, wherein also ye are risen with him through the faith of the operation of God, who hath raised him from the dead* (Colossians 2:10-12).

We need to take this literally. If we are as Jesus is now, what does that look like? Well, what quality of life does Jesus now enjoy? Jesus is now King of kings. Jesus took all sickness and disease on the cross and conquered it, so He is forever free from them. Jesus has already faced death and hell and beaten them, so He has no fear of death. Jesus is united with His Father and is currently experiencing a good relationship with His family. Jesus has the satisfaction of knowing that He was sent on a mission and completed every aspect of it to the fullest extent. He has the right to feel complete in knowing that He finished His course. The list could go on and on, but I think you get the idea. The same quality of life that Jesus now enjoys, He won for us on the cross.

In fact, the Greek word for this kind of life is *sozo*, which refers not just to the state of being alive but to a certain quality of life. Because of what Jesus did for us on the cross, we not only have His life in us but we also have it at the same quality He has it. *Sozo* denotes that the person receiving the life will experience the same quality as the giver of that life. If we are as Jesus is, that means we have the same quality of life in us that Jesus has.

> *The same quality of life that Jesus now enjoys, He won for us on the cross.*

Let me ask you a question. You may know that you are saved and are on your way to heaven, but are you experiencing the same kind of life Jesus is right now? You may believe in it intellectually, but are you experiencing it? To "believe" in this sense means to be fully persuaded with no doubt. So often our problem is that, even when we believe and know what is in us, opposing doubts arise at the same time.

Look inside yourself. When you read that you can experience the same kind of life Jesus has, what happened inside you? How did your heart respond? Did you say, "I know that!"? Did you say, "This is amazing! I had no idea Jesus did that for me!"? Did you say, "I can't have that quality of life because I have done such and such a sin"?

In one way or another, all those responses contain unbelief. We tend to think of things in terms of black and white;

we either believe or we don't believe. The point I'm making is this: Unbelief creeps into our hearts in varying ways and to varying degrees. Our pride would lead us to assume that we fully believe God and we might even get offended if someone suggested otherwise. That response is in itself unbelief. If you were truly persuaded in godly matters, then these kinds of ideas would have no effect; you would rise above them easily.

I'm not attempting to create a sense of lack in you or make you feel guilty for not experiencing all God has for you because I am in the same boat. All I'm trying to do is drive home the point that all our problems boil down essentially to one simple issue: unbelief. I make this point in order to instill hope. I make this point in order to simplify the struggles we face. We don't have to worry about the devil or about confessing the right scripture enough times; all we have to do is believe. We don't have to pray the perfect prayer or try to find the narrow road of God for our lives. If we will simply believe and trust the Lord, He will work everything out.

Believing God is the answer to all our problems. Whenever you are faced with an issue, struggle, temptation or sin, simply ask yourself, "Am I believing God right now?" If you'll do that, God's ability will come alive in your heart and you will overcome. You will begin to experience that quality of life that Jesus provided.

## JESUS GAVE US EVERYTHING WE NEED

You might be thinking, *Clint, that's just not practical. How am I supposed to simply "believe God"?* Have you ever really thought about what it means to "believe God" in every situation? "Just believe God, brother" has become a cliché in many Christian circles, but it's the advice we all need to hear when we have lost our way. So then, how *do* we believe God? How do we get to the point where we are fully persuaded? That's the tricky part.

> *There remaineth therefore a rest to the people of God. For he that is entered into his rest, he also hath ceased from his own works, as God did from his. Let us labour therefore to enter into that rest, lest any man fall after the same example of unbelief* (Hebrews 4:9-11).

The "labor" we partake of to enter God's rest is composed of the very things we have come to believe make up the Christian life: praying, reading the Bible, going to church, listening to God, confessing Scripture...the list goes on and on. All these things are good and necessary, but why do we do them? What is our *real* motivation? Do we do them to feel accepted by God? Do we do them from a sense of obligation? Do we do them because we've been told that's what Christians are supposed to do?

The obvious answer to all these questions is no. So here's a trickier one: Do we do these things to *receive* from God? The truth is, if we have Jesus, then we already have everything God is ever going to give us in this life. When we accepted Jesus, we got everything that we could possibly get.

Colossians 2:9 says that all the fullness of the Godhead dwells bodily in Jesus. If we have Jesus in us, we have the fullness of God. There is nothing left for God to give. So then, what is the acceptable answer as to why we should do all these good things? The answer is twofold. First of all, we should do them in order to deepen our relationship with God out of a desire to know Him more. Through these actions we press into Him because we know that He loves us and because we want to know more about just how much He loves us.

*If we have Jesus, then we have everything God can give us.*

Secondly, we do those things to persuade ourselves of the truth. We should labor to enter into the rest that comes from being fully persuaded that we are complete in Him. The next time you confess a scripture, ask yourself if you are expecting God to do something or if you are persuading yourself to believe that you already have it. God is not going to do one more thing for you in this life. He already has done everything. Are you expecting your prayers to convince God to move on your behalf?

Sometimes when I tell people these truths they think I'm saying that prayer is not valuable. That's not what I'm saying at all. Prayer is a gift from God and we are supposed to pray. I'm just saying that when we pray we need to check our motivation. If you pray expecting God to "do" something, then you are walking in unbelief. God may help you understand how to connect with what He's already given you or lead you in a direction that will allow you to see His provision, but you don't have to convince Him to do anything for you. Someone once said that prayer is not overcoming God's reluctance but laying hold of His willingness.

Prayer does change things, but it usually changes us, not God. In healing, prayer connects a sick person to what God has already put in him or her. God is not sitting up there in heaven deciding who to heal and who not to heal. We are like God in the sense that our words can go forth and create situations or have a positive effect on people. He created us that way. The reality is that when we begin to speak God's life over our bodies and see ourselves being made whole, we are exercising what God has already put in us. God is not swooping down and deciding to heal our bodies. I'm not saying that we heal ourselves, but that God put His life in us so that we can connect to it and experience it at all times. If we get healed or experience a miracle it is because of what Jesus did for us. On this side of the cross, we don't have to convince God to do for us what He has already done.

Once again, the choice is yours. Will you choose to walk in Satan's secret sin of unbelief and continue to live a life far below the abundant life Jesus died to give you, or will you believe God and embrace what He has already placed in you and, in that assurance, reach out and claim the fullness of life you were meant to live?

Ultimately, it boils down to a very simple choice: Will you live according to *lies* or will you live according to the *truth*?

# Chapter Eleven

# THE TRUTH VS. THE LIE

⊷ ⌖◊⌖ ⊶

Pontius Pilate asked Jesus, "What is truth?" People have been asking that question and searching for the answer ever since Adam and Eve got kicked out of Eden. The quest for truth is a universal drive. Everybody wants to know the truth. Even in an age where more and more people are questioning whether there is any such thing as objective truth, deep down inside they, too, want to know that some things are absolute.

So then, what *is* truth? Many people equate truth with reality; they think whatever is real is true. But that raises another question: What is reality? Are truth and reality the same?

Actually, truth and reality are quite different. Reality can be defined as all of our experiences that determine how things appear to us. By this definition, my reality may be different from yours depending on our personal backgrounds,

141

experiences and perspectives. That doesn't sound much like truth, which is supposed to be unchanging. If you want a good perspective on how "reality" depends upon the observer, just try reading the reports filed by several witnesses to the same automobile accident! Our reality is colored by the perspective from which we approach our circumstances. It is our interpretation of what is happening around us at any given moment. We can say we live in reality, but do we live in the truth?

*Truth and reality are quite different.*

Truth, on the other hand, can be defined as a fact that has been verified. Scientists love this definition. Verified facts don't change. They can be relied upon to be the same today as they were yesterday and the same tomorrow as they were today. You can set your watch by truth. You can bet your life on truth because it will never change.

Our reality is constantly changing. Have you ever read a sentence that didn't make sense and then reread it over and over? Maybe one word in the sentence doesn't seem to fit. Finally you realize that you were misreading that word. You read the word but somehow your mind saw a different word. Once you read the sentence correctly, it changes the whole meaning. Your original "reality" has been adjusted by correct information. Or perhaps you were offended by something someone said only to realize later that you heard that person wrong. Again, your reality changed to fit a new situation. Have you ever been alone in a dark house and been frightened by a strange sound? You just knew that there was someone in the house, but it was only a cat or a tree limb rubbing against a window.

In all these situations the experienced emotions were real even though the situation wasn't true. You may have really been offended to the point where you started to feel angry or experience a headache or something else. It's real to you, but the truth of the situation is something completely different.

Our minds have the ability to create a reality. At the top of our spinal cord is a small bundle of nerves called the Reticular Activating System (RAS). An interesting phenomenon occurs that is related to the RAS. When we observe something and assume that we know what is really happening, our RAS kicks in and begins to narrow our thought processes down, helping us rule out other options. In a sense, the RAS works with us to prove that we are right. Our bodies, in turn, respond chemically by producing the appropriate chemicals so that what we are convinced of biologically is now reinforced emotionally.

The only problem with this is that if our initial judgment was wrong, then we have set ourselves on a course that is totally untrue even though it is our reality. I believe God created the RAS so that we could focus on Him and rule out all lies and hindrances that could cause us to stray from Him. But, like every other good thing God gave us, we have learned how to corrupt it and turn it to our own selfish purposes.

Reality is what we make it. Our perception is our reality. Truth, on the other hand, is God's perception. Truth is absolute. Reality is subjective; it changes constantly. For example, I was watching TV one day and saw a commercial that showed cars racing on a dirt road. The volume was low enough that I could not hear the sound. My first impression—my reality—was that it was an ad for an upcoming race. As I looked closer, however, I noticed that the cars did not look quite right. As it turned out, I was watching a commercial for a new video game. The graphics were so good that at first glance the cars looked real. But they weren't real. Although my reality at the beginning was that I was watching real cars, the truth was that I was watching video game graphics. We may accept a reality that is completely off base from the truth.

## TRUTH VS. REALITY

After telling people about my experience, I am always asked if I still think that what happened to me was real. My answer is always yes. The problem is that my experience was not all based on truth. The truth of the situation is that through the use of LSD my awareness was such that I was able to hear and communicate with demonic beings. Demons are real and if we put ourselves in the right positions, we will begin to hear them. My reality was that I had died and gone to hell, but that wasn't the truth.

The truth was that I was totally convinced of the lies that these demons, as well as Satan himself, told me. Even though I wasn't dead and in hell, I fully believed that I was because that was the reality that I allowed to be created. At any moment I could have changed my reality to align with truth, but the problem was that I didn't know the truth.

Having the ability to create our own reality is an incredible gift, but there is one catch. If our reality is not based on the truth, then we are off course. My reality got so off course that I thought I was dead when I was really very much alive. This is how people can convince themselves of anything. If we start with something we think is close enough to the truth and create our reality based on what we're experiencing, but never check to see if we're staying with truth, we will eventually lose the truth altogether.

As an example, consider two cars starting in Atlanta, Georgia, and driving to Los Angeles, California. Both cars start off on the same path, but one is just ever so slightly off by a fraction of a degree. At the beginning of the journey both cars are on the right course, but by the time they reach California, the car that was only slightly off course is now miles away from its target.

That is what happens to us. We start out with the truth, but by turning slightly we end up in a reality that we never thought we could reach. If someone had told me beforehand that one day I was going to believe that I was dead when I was really alive, I would have laughed in his face.

Due to the choices I made and the lies I believed along the way, my mind was in a place where it could actually accept that reality. This happens to some degree in all our lives. The good news is that we can bring ourselves back to the truth. We can stray as far as possible, but God's truth is so reliable that the moment we look back to it we can snap out of our reality and back into truth.

The problem with the world is that they don't know the truth. Lost people and even many Christians don't know the truth. After 2,000 years, the teaching and preaching of Christianity have deviated in some places and times until today some so-called "Christian" groups are steeped in error and two-thirds of the world's population are going to hell.

How could our world be so off track? It's because we live in our comfortable realities and don't align ourselves with

God's truth. How has your life and perception deviated from the truth you know? It's not always easy to change our perceptions, but we must do whatever it takes to make our reality line up with God's truth.

*We must do whatever it takes to make our reality line up with God's truth.*

And what is God's truth? God's truth is that all His promises are yes and amen. God's truth is that all our needs are met according to His riches in glory in Christ Jesus. God's truth is that Jesus paid the price for all our guilt, sorrow, pain and sickness. God's truth is that sin has no more dominion over us. God's truth is that we are a new creation. God's truth is that life is easy and light. Are you experiencing God's truth or just your reality?

## A TOOTHLESS LION

Some of the other statements and questions that usually arise when I tell the story of my experience with the devil are, "That's unbelievable!" "What was real and what wasn't?" "Are you saying that the devil can make people believe whatever he wants?" The number one thing I hear is that the whole thing was just in my head. Most people, for whatever reason, simply can't accept that something like this can even happen.

My response is multifaceted. I tell this story not to glorify the devil or to make people afraid of him. I tell this story to expose the truth. And what is that truth? The truth revealed from my experience is that *the devil has no bite whatsoever*. He's all bark but no bite. First Peter 5:8 says that our adversary, the devil, walks about like a roaring lion, seeking someone to devour. Thanks to the work of Christ on the cross, who came to destroy the works of the devil (1 John 3:8), if the devil is a lion, he's a toothless lion. The only people he can devour are those who are careless enough or ignorant enough of the truth (like I was) to allow it.

The devil's secret weapons are manipulation and confusion, but they are rendered useless in the light of God's power working within the human heart. As Mick Jagger of The Rolling Stones said in the song "Sympathy for the Devil," "What's confusing you is the nature of my game." Satan has no other power. The Bible is very clear about the true nature of the devil: He is a powerless loser, a liar and the father of lies. Speaking of the devil, Jesus said this:

*...He was a murderer from the beginning, and abode not in the truth, because there is no truth in him. When he speaketh a lie, he speaketh of his own: for he is a liar, and the father of it* (John 8:44).

The reason my experience seems unreal to many people is that they don't think their situation could ever go to such an extreme. We all tend to be comfortable with our level of awareness. Substance abusers who hear my story might tell themselves that their lives would never spin that far out of control. Addicts of any kind always tell themselves that their addiction will never lead them to the point of death. Sinners staunchly stand behind the belief that their sin could never bring them to the place where they turn their back on God and come face to face with the devil.

The truth is, I was not dead and I was not in hell. Granted, there were several occasions during that period of time when my life could have ended, but neither Satan nor any of the demons who tormented me for so long had the power to kill me. For all his arrogance and cool demeanor, Satan turned out to be a toothless lion.

How could this have been so real to me? How could I have believed for months that I was dead and in hell? How is it possible that the human mind could have that kind of capacity? While I was going through it, no one could have convinced me that it was not real.

Not even God could help me until I was ready to help myself. Until I reached a place where I was fed up enough or angry enough or miserable enough to decide to do something about it, there was little God could do. This is not to say that God is powerless; not at all. I firmly believe that He was involved, putting people or situations in my path that helped me turn toward Him, but until I exercised my free will to turn to Him, He could only do so much. Free will is the key. God gave us free will, and He never violates it. We are not robots. God never makes us do anything against our will. He gave us all the capacity to choose life or death.

*Free will is the key.*

In my case, the LSD opened my mind to the dark side of the spiritual realm and, as he did with Jesus in the desert, Satan attacked at my weakest point. At the very moment the drug was at its peak in my body, the devil decided to make his move. This is one of the devil's favorite tactics; he moves in when we are at our weakest. He tries to take advantage of the instability of our thinking or the weakness of our emotions. Satan does not have the power to plant thoughts into our minds or even to read our minds, but he is a master at reading weakness, and that's where he strikes.

## LIVING IN TWO WORLDS

The devil is a fallen angel; he is therefore a spiritual being. Man is a three-part being: body, soul (mind) and spirit. Because we are part spirit, we are connected to the spiritual realm. We tend to think of eternity and even heaven and hell as being some "place." This is inconsistent with the concepts of eternity. We exist and function within the frame of space and time, but we also are connected to eternity. We are partly spirit so there is a part of us that exists in the eternal realm.

This makes us able to communicate with God, who is Spirit, but it also makes us able to be in touch with every aspect of the spiritual realm. In response to people who say that my experience was in my head, that is partly true. My brain ultimately did process what was happening, but it was my spirit that first picked up on the evil that was ensuing around me.

When we are reborn in Christ, our spirit has been made new, and we are regenerated. We are literally made one with God through Jesus Christ. Our spirit is made up of the same substance as God. In John 17, Jesus prays that we become one as He and the Father are one. That prayer was fulfilled when Jesus rose from the dead and God sent His Holy Spirit to live within us.

Up until that point, the Holy Spirit would temporarily come upon people. But it was not until after the resurrection of Jesus that He took up permanent residence in people's hearts. Jesus said just before He died that He had to return to the Father so the Holy Spirit could come. Why was the coming of the Holy Spirit so important? Our spirits needed to be regenerated so that God could live in our hearts. The

Bible tells us that because of Christ, the kingdom of heaven is now within us through the Holy Spirit.

The difference for the believer in communicating with the spiritual realm is that we communicate with God who is *in* us as opposed to outside us as in the case of fallen spiritual beings. Demonic beings are *not* inside us; they never are. Throughout my experience, I never once had beings inside of me. I was possessed, but not in the way most Christians understand the term.

*Thayer's Greek Lexicon* defines possession as being "under the power of," not being indwelt by.[1] We have been taught that demonic possession is when a demon takes our bodies by living inside of us, but that is not true. That may be the apparent reality, but it is not truth. It's just like alcohol: We can become drunk being under the influence of alcohol, but alcohol never takes over our body. It has an effect on our body, but it never takes the place of our blood or our bodily fluids. It merely acts on them. The same is true with demonic possession. We can bring ourselves to the place where we become thoroughly consumed by the lies and doctrines of demons, but we always have the choice whether or not to believe and act on that influence.

Every person I have ever dealt with who claimed to be possessed admits to having a point of choice and a degree of control throughout the entire process. So how does the devil create so much influence over our lives? First of all, we have to be at a place where we are looking for something outside of God to fill a life need. This will usually show in our

---

1. *Thayer's Greek Definitions*, Ed. 3 (Cedar Rapids, Iowa: Parson's Technology, Inc.), Electronic Edition STEP Files, 1999, Findex.com, Inc.

actions. The fallen world picks up on this and makes its move. I can't explain exactly how that operates, but the Bible does confirm that the devil comes to steal, kill and destroy. At the point of attack, because we are partly spirit, we can "hear" the devil and demonic beings.

When we look outside of ourselves to fill a need and start to listen to the lies of devils, we make the choice whether or not to believe them. That's not to say that anytime we are not hearing God we are hearing the devil, but the possibility is there.

## SATAN: A CONQUERED ENEMY

Now let me give you the good news. Anytime we find ourselves looking for an option that originates in the demonic realm, God is right there reminding us what He has done for us. How many times have you wanted to sin and heard a scripture inside you or started to hear a worship song that you shoved back down? That was God trying to get you to connect to His power and overcome that temptation.

The temptation is not even from the devil. The devil is so limited in power that he can't even create temptation. James 1:14 says, *"But every man is tempted, when he is drawn away of his own lust, and enticed."* In reality, we set up our own temptations by our willingness to listen to our own lusts and the urges of our fallen nature.

So now that we've taken away Satan's ability to possess us and his ability to tempt us and his ability to read our minds or put thoughts in our minds, what's left? What's left is our own foolishness. What's left is our own willingness to follow him. What's left is exactly what Jesus faced and conquered back in that desert. Jesus was not possessed by the devil, but the possibility was there. Jesus audibly heard Satan, He saw what Satan wanted Him to see, yet He didn't give in. That is how we are supposed to handle an encounter with the devil.

We should not be shocked if the devil tries to mount an attack, but we also should take great comfort that Jesus has already dealt with this situation and *Through Jesus,* conquered it. The Bible tells us that Jesus was tempted in every way *we have the* that we are tempted. Jesus could have given up His will to Satan and *fullness of* fallen into possession, but He didn't. *God in us!* Jesus was more convinced of what was in Him than of what the devil was showing Him. The devil presented an option that looked like Jesus' goal, but Jesus knew that He would be compromising His identity if He had attained the goal that way.

You might say, "Well, that's Jesus, but what about me?" Scripturally, there is no difference. Colossians tells us that all the fullness of the Godhead dwelled bodily within Jesus. Through the Holy Spirit, Jesus now lives inside of us, which means that we have all the fullness of God within us! If we fall because of what the devil tells us, we are simply choosing to believe his lie.

Here's an illustration I like to use. All of us know what it is like to try to talk to someone who is so engrossed in watching TV that he or she doesn't even hear us. And all of us are equally guilty of doing the same thing. The person we're trying to talk to seems to be ignoring us. In a way the person is, but more accurately, his or her attention is so focused on what he or she is watching that he or she simply does not hear us and may not even be aware of our presence.

That's the way we are with demons. They can come and shout their lies, but we should be so focused on God that we don't even notice their presence. That's the key: *focusing on God*. James 4:7-8a says, *"Submit yourselves therefore to God. Resist the devil, and he will flee from you. Draw nigh to God, and he will draw nigh to you."* If by chance we do turn our attention toward the demons and their lies, we should know immediately that what we're hearing is ungodly and turn away. If that doesn't help, our hearts have been renewed and have the capability of bringing to our remembrance our true identity in Christ. And if *that* doesn't bring us back on track, the Holy Spirit is inside us saying, "You are righteous; you don't have to listen to that. You don't have to entertain that option."

So, basically, if we fall or believe something negative about ourselves, we have turned our back on who we are in Christ, we have turned our back on our own hearts and we've turned our back on the Holy Spirit who is always with us trying to help us. We have to totally go against our nature and God to believe a lie from the devil—a lie that may be telling us we are sick or worthless or unlovable or dead or in hell or anything else that is contrary to what God has told us in His Word about our new identity. When we choose to believe a lie of the devil, we go against everything that we are.

Such is the power of the devil. Satan is keenly aware that we do not fully believe that we are who God says we are. He knows that in general we are more comfortable validating our own identity than looking to God for His validation of our identity. We do not come under the influence of the devil by his mighty power because he has none. We come under the influence of the devil when we choose to call God a liar and call Satan the father of truth. That may be a strong statement, but it's a true statement. Satan is the father of lies and our God is the Father of truth, righteousness and holiness.

## THE DEVIL IS A LOSER

When we accept Christ, we become as righteous and as holy as Jesus Himself, not because of anything we have done but because of what He did for us on the cross. We are the righteousness of God in Christ Jesus and we have no business stepping outside of our new identity and choosing to believe a lie of some insignificant, fallen, lying devil. The devil is the weakest being in existence. Anyone who relies on the weakness of others in order to triumph is a loser, and true losers never win.

The devil is a total loser and has no power in your life. The Bible tells us that when we get to heaven we will look at the devil and be astonished that we could have ever been afraid of such a powerless creature.

*They that see thee shall narrowly look upon thee, and consider thee, saying, Is this the man that made the earth to tremble, that did shake kingdoms; that made the world as a wilderness, and destroyed the cities thereof; that opened not the house of his prisoners?* (Isaiah 14:16-17)

Contrary to popular opinion, the devil cannot make you "do it." The devil will take you as far as you let him. He will do everything he can to ruin your life. He will lie to you, lead you to cheat on your spouse, bring you into compromising situations and even kill you, but he can do those things *only* with your permission.

Decide today that you will never again fear the devil's power in your life. Decide today that you will never again choose to believe his lies. Decide today that you will always choose to believe God when He has done everything He can do to give you a new nature and a way to connect to Him eternally. Live the rest of your life with a sense of empowerment knowing that the devil is not a factor for you to fear.

# Chapter Twelve

# CHOOSE LIFE

＋·‐ ≊◆≊ ‐·＋

Earlier in my story, I mentioned the issue of choice. Several times in my experience I could have chosen to turn to God or question what I was hearing, but I never did. I chose death. Choice is a powerful thing. Through circumstances and erroneous beliefs, we often think that our hands are tied. We lead ourselves to think we have no choices. As far out of my mind as I was, I knew I still had choices. I could have turned everything around, but I didn't know how. I am not going to point fingers at anyone for the fact that I knew nothing about God, but that is the one and only reason I did not stop my hellish ride when it began. God loves us so much—and wanted us to love Him freely in return—that He gave us the power to choose for ourselves. When we choose Him, the rewards are unimaginable.

*I call heaven and earth to record this day against you, that I have set before you life and death, blessing and cursing: therefore choose life, that both thou and thy seed may live: that thou mayest love the LORD thy God, and that thou mayest obey his voice, and that thou mayest cleave unto him: for he is thy life, and the length of thy days: that thou mayest dwell in the land which the LORD sware unto thy fathers, to Abraham, to Isaac, and to Jacob, to give them* (Deuteronomy 30:19-20).

*Choice is a powerful thing.*

God has given us a free will, which allows us to be creative beings. This free will allows for biblical decisions as well as decisions to sin. We have the freedom to do whatever we want. God has given us guidelines to make sound decisions and have success, but He does not decide for us in advance what we are going to choose. He knows what we will choose, but He does not decide for us.

When we get saved, God does not just assign us a particular road to take and then leave us to figure out through some spooky means exactly what it is we are supposed to be doing in life. God will and does call us to very specific tasks, but we do not just go through life in some weird pre-planned path that we have no control over. We are not robots. God has made us one with Him, putting His Spirit in us through the blood of Jesus, but we are still separate, intelligent souls. God has expressed His love in many ways, but free will is one of the greatest because it demonstrates trust, which is essential for true love.

Giving us free will yet equipping us with His Word is God's plan for real success. When we make the conscious decision to trust God in life, we open ourselves up to His wisdom and unfailing guidance.

*Trust in the LORD with all thine heart; and lean not unto thine own understanding. In all thy ways acknowledge him, and he shall direct thy paths. Be not wise in thine own eyes: fear the LORD, and depart from evil* (Proverbs 3:5-7).

The Bible is God's road map for success. More than just an instruction guide for how to get to heaven, the Bible is also a handbook on how to live successfully now on this earth. The longer I live as a believer, the more convinced I am that we are in control of where we will go and through the power of God's grace and Word, He will always be there to help us in our decisions. He has not abandoned us here to fend for ourselves but has given us all wisdom through Jesus. I love the fact that God is a father and has fatherly wisdom for us in His revealed Word.

I used to think that God had a specific plan for my life that entailed making the one right decision in all situations. This caused much frustration, especially when it came to the smallest decisions. On top of that, I believed that this life was already planned out for me, that I was predestined. The combination of these two false truths left me very confused. I thought that even if I did make a decision that seemed wrong, it had to be part of God's plan. This thinking led me to the point where I believed that no matter what I did, God already had everything planned out, so it didn't really matter what I did. Why read the Bible or pray if everything is predetermined?

Well, I finally discovered that I was not a robot. I learned that I could make wrong decisions that caused pain and death. I knew pain wasn't from God, so I must have brought it on myself. I also discovered that when I based decisions on the Word of God, I would come out victorious even if I had not "felt" God telling me to do something. Every opportunity was out there for me to succeed. There did not have to be just one right decision for every situation. Through obeying the moral will of God, not to be righteous but to stop hurting, I found that it *did* matter what decisions I made. God has given us the guidelines to make sound decisions, but it is up to us to believe Him and act accordingly. We have received Jesus, but we also need to walk in the new nature that He died to give us.

*It is up to us to believe God and act accordingly.*

One of the most amazing things that Jesus accomplished was making us one with God, putting His Spirit in us through His blood. We are one with our Father, but we still retain our individual personalities. Our spirit is one with our heavenly Father's. We now have a new nature and a new life source within us. As 2 Corinthians 5:17 says, we are new creatures in Christ. We have new hearts empowered by God's Spirit. Through this divine life in us, we can now walk and live with the same degree of success that Jesus had. Realizing this is important for our confidence in our decision-making abilities. God wants us to know and believe that we are new creatures with the power to live and decide victoriously in this life.

Having God's life in us affects our minds and renews them to the way they were originally created to function. Of course, we can still make harmful decisions, but now we have God's life in us to lead us toward success. The leading of the Holy Spirit does not have to be some mystical thing.

God's life in us is very real and very personal and very practical. We do not have to look outside of ourselves for God or to some outside circumstance. The God-life that is in us continually is always leading us into success. All we have to do is follow and obey. When we believe this and make sound decisions based on the Word of God, we will have victory. As long as we are honest with ourselves in the decisions we make and base them on the Word of God, we can be confident that we are in the will of God.

I no longer fear missing a narrow road that I think God has laid out for me. God is big enough to allow us to have options and help us in whatever decision we make. I do not have to find the one correct decision in all situations. I can thank God in some cases for having choices. I know God calls us to specific tasks and places, but even then, we still have freedom of choice. God called me to the church I presently attend, but I could go somewhere else if I chose to.

God wants us to choose life and walk in success, but He left it up to us to decide what path to take. We're not supposed to figure out God's decisions for us but allow God to influence our decision-making. He is there to give us wisdom, but He also wants us to use the awesome decision-making power that He gave us. He has made us truly and completely free.

Our freedom to choose is another facet of His love for us. If God had created a bunch of robots with no decision-making power, there would have been perfect obedience but no love. God wants to receive glory and honor and praise from beings who offer it freely from loving hearts. God is love and wants nothing but to express His love and have that love expressed back to Him. His ultimate act of love was sending

Jesus to die for us. When we make the free will decision to believe and express our gratitude and love toward Him freely in return, God receives glory.

Realizing that God has given us the freedom to choose life or death makes me appreciate His love even more. I challenge you today to choose life. No matter where you've been or what you've done, God can save you. Choose life. The way of the world is the way of the devil and leads only to death. Choose life.

*Choose life.*

Perhaps you have never known this God-life I have been talking about. Perhaps you don't know what it means to trust Jesus as your Savior and receive forgiveness for your sins and the gift of the Holy Spirit to make the God-life a reality in you. If you do not know this life, you can. It's easy. Simply repeat the prayer below and then read the New Testament in the Bible.

"God, I am willing to try it Your way. I believe that You sent Jesus as a man to take the punishment for my sin. While Jesus hung on that cross, You put the judgment for all sin on Him. He died and went to hell in my place. You raised Him from the dead, bringing Him back to You. I can spend eternity with You because of this. You then sent the Holy Spirit to live in me. Jesus, I accept You as my personal Savior and as my righteousness. I am acceptable to God because of You. I am righteous and perfect now because of You. I believe that the Holy Spirit is in me now. Teach me how to walk in Your strength and love. Thank You for creating the plan of salvation so I can forever have a love relationship with You."

If you prayed that prayer, please contact me on the web at www.clintbyars.com. I look forward to hearing from you!

# THE TRUTH VS. THE LIE

*The lie is... There is no God.*

The truth is... "The fool hath said in his heart, There is no God" (Psalm 14:1).

*The lie is... God does not love you.*

The truth is... "But God commendeth his love toward us, in that, while we were yet sinners, Christ died for us" (Romans 5:8).

*The lie is... God's holding out on you.*

The truth is... "He that spared not his own Son, but delivered him up for us all, how shall he not with him also freely give us all things?" (Romans 8:32)

*The lie is… Satan has power over you.*

The truth is… "Submit yourselves therefore to God. Resist the devil, and he will flee from you" (James 4:7).

*The lie is… God's lying to you.*

The truth is… "For all the promises of God in him are yea, and in him Amen, unto the glory of God by us" (2 Corinthians 1:20).

*The lie is… God has abandoned you.*

The truth is… "For he hath said, I will never leave thee, nor forsake thee" (Hebrews 13:5b).

*The lie is… God cannot help you.*

The truth is… "Fear thou not; for I am with thee: be not dismayed; for I am thy God: I will strengthen thee; yea, I will help thee; yea, I will uphold thee with the right hand of my righteousness" (Isaiah 41:10).

*The lie is… You've sinned too much for God to save you.*

The truth is… "For whosoever shall call upon the name of the Lord shall be saved" (Romans 10:13).

*The lie is… God doesn't care about you.*

The truth is… "Casting all your care upon him; for he careth for you" (1 Peter 5:7).

*The lie is... You have no hope.*

The truth is... "To whom God would make known what is the riches of the glory of this mystery among the Gentiles; which is Christ in you, the hope of glory" (Colossians 1:27).

*The lie is... Don't bother to pray; God won't listen to you.*

The truth is... "For I know the thoughts that I think toward you, saith the LORD, thoughts of peace, and not of evil, to give you an expected end. Then shall ye call upon me, and ye shall go and pray unto me, and I will hearken unto you. And ye shall seek me, and find me, when ye shall search for me with all your heart" (Jeremiah 29:11-13).

*The lie is... You can't be forgiven.*

The truth is... "There is therefore now no condemnation to them which are in Christ Jesus, who walk not after the flesh, but after the Spirit" (Romans 8:1).

*The lie is... You can't escape your past.*

The truth is... "Therefore if any man be in Christ, he is a new creature: old things are passed away; behold, all things are become new" (2 Corinthians 5:17).

*The lie is... God won't take care of you.*

The truth is... "But my God shall supply all your need according to his riches in glory by Christ Jesus" (Philippians 4:19).

*The lie is... Being a Christian will be hard and miserable.*

The truth is... "Come unto me, all ye that labour and are heavy laden, and I will give you rest. Take my yoke upon you, and learn of me; for I am meek and lowly in heart: and ye shall find rest unto your souls. For my yoke is easy, and my burden is light" (Matthew 11:28-30).

*The lie is... You have to work for your salvation.*

The truth is... "For by grace are ye saved through faith; and that not of yourselves: it is the gift of God: not of works, lest any man should boast" (Ephesians 2:8-9).

*The lie is... Your sins will always control you.*

The truth is... "For the law of the Spirit of life in Christ Jesus hath made me free from the law of sin and death" (Romans 8:2).

# ABOUT THE AUTHOR

Clint Byars is an associate pastor at Impact of Huntsville church in Huntsville, Alabama. He also teaches at Impact International School of Ministry and serves as a counselor. As a former youth pastor, Clint saw much success in building teenagers in the confidence of who they are in Christ. He holds a bachelor's degree in theology.

Clint and his wife Sara own and operate Glory Graphics, which produces Glory Gear Clothing, a Christian-themed apparel company. They have two children, Sydney and Reese.

# Personal Journal

# Personal Journal

# Personal Journal

# Personal Journal

---
---
---
---
---
---
---
---
---
---
---
---
---
---
---
---
---
---
---
---
---
---
---
---
---
---
---

# Personal Journal